Emma Hamilton

Emma Hamilton

Julie Peakman

HAUS PUBLISHING • LONDON

First published in Great Britain in 2005 by
Haus Publishing Limited
26 Cadogan Court
London SW3 3BX

Copyright © Julie Peakman, 2005

The moral right of the author has been asserted

A CIP catalogue record for this book
is available from the British Library

ISBN 1-904341-98-5 (paperback)

Designed and typeset in Garamond
Printed and bound by Graphicom in Vicenza, Italy

Front cover: Emma *Bacchante* a stipple engraving by Charles Knight after
George Romney. Courtesy Bridgeman Art Library
Back cover: Emma as Circe by George Romney. Courtesy akg-Images

Contents

Introduction

Emma Hamilton has always been a controversial figure in history. Her story is the classic tale of an 18th-century woman's rise from poverty to fame and riches using nothing but her talent, wits and determination. Yet lurid tales have been associated with her, thanks to her drunkenness, her alleged lasciviousness and her contrived airs. Her detractors have depicted her as a hanger-on, a bore, a melodramatic poseur and a self-seeking opportunist, but how much of this is true? Was she a schemer or was she merely at the right place at the right time, merely happening to become the lover of the greatest naval hero of all time? Was her self-sacrificing image based on real generosity of spirit or merely Emma creating her own image as a career move? Emma's admirers point to her artistic leanings, her wonderful voice and her charming personality; but others have held that her voice jarred and she came across as vulgar and fat. Emma had been described as 'at best a rather silly woman' who 'bought little dignity to her husband's career and ended by becoming rather ridiculous'.[1] But this rather denies Emma's shrewdness; although without much formal education, Emma was undoubtedly intelligent, and clever enough to use whatever means possible to gain access to the world she wanted.

Amy Lyon (as Emma was christened) was brought up to be a respectable working-class girl. Beautiful and vivacious, she was a 'fallen woman' in her youth, excluded from respectable society after an early affair. Packed off to Naples when her 'protector' tired of her, there by exploiting her natural talents she rose to become a titled lady and the toast of Neapolitan society, wielding political influence as the close friend and confidante of Queen Maria Carolina. She was adored by two of the most famous men of the 18th century. First mistress, then wife, to Sir William Hamilton, she went on to capture the heart of the most renowned sea-fighter of all time, Horatio Nelson. For more than five years she was involved in a strange *ménage à trois* which scandalised London.

The love affair between Emma Hamilton and Nelson is one of the most talked about relationships of all time. Nelson saw her as 'his wife before God', his 'Alpha and Omega',[2] while for Emma, Nelson was to become *the dearest husband of my heart*.[3] Although they were never to spend more than four whole years together, Nelson was the love of Emma's life. When they met, Emma was already married to the British Envoy to Naples, Sir William Hamilton, known for his glittering diplomatic career and price-less collection of classical antiquities. Hamilton appears to have tolerated the affair taking place under his own roof, and on their return to England, after Emma had given birth to Nelson's child, Hamilton would continue to live with her, both of them moving into Nelson's house at Merton. The three of them called them-selves the *Tria juncta in uno* (three in one) in joking reference to the motto of the Knights of the Order of the Bath which both Sir William and Nelson belonged. But what led them to be able to maintain a domestic situation which would be unacceptable to most men? What possessed Emma to endanger all she had gained by her marriage to Sir William in order to keep both her husband and her lover? Most curious was the deep affection and respect between Sir William and Horatio Nelson which enabled them to share the woman they both loved.

However, Emma should not just be remembered for her mar-riage to Hamilton and her affair with Nelson, but also for her own achievements. Rising from poverty to become an educated and influential woman, she played an important part in diplomatic affairs at Naples, helping to influence the Queen to support the British in the Mediterranean at the height of the French Revolutionary War. Resolute and ambitious, she yearned for glory, much as Nelson himself did. Despite her fondness for melodramatics, it was observed by her contemporaries that she stood firm in the face of danger. Her opportunity came when she was able to intercept secret letters and pass them on to the British government, and also helped organise the escape of the Royal Family from Naples, so that Maria Carolina avoided the fate of her unfortunate sister, Marie Antoinette of France.

Throughout her life, Emma was loyal to her family and friends, and was not frightened to do what she felt was right whatever the consequences to herself. She wrote to Nelson at the beginning of their relationship: *I would not be a lukewarm friend for the world. I cannot make friends with all but the few friends I have I would die for them.*[4] Yet many of those she cared for would exploit her kindness, and in the end abandon her.

This is a story of a young woman who could easily have ended up as another discarded mistress, descending the well-worn path to prostitution and disease. Yet she was able to recover much of her reputation and achieve wealth and the chance of fame through her marriage to Sir William Hamilton, only to put it all in danger for the love of Nelson.

Early Years

The future Emma Hamilton was born Amy Lyon on 26 April 1765 and baptised on 12 May in the parish church at Ness in South Wirral, and as a child was called Emy, Emly and Emily. Although Emma always gave this as her birthday, it is possible she was born earlier (Jeaffreson gives 1761 and Gruffyd gives 1763, although neither provide evidence). This may have been altered to conceal her illegitimacy as her parents did not marry until 1764; Jeaffreson suggests she was four years old when she was baptised.[5] Neston, the town of her birth, was one of the most important and populous places in the area thanks to the opening of Ness Colliery in 1750. Men from all over the area came in search of work and her father, Henry Lyon, found employment as a blacksmith.

Emma's parents married in Ness on 11 June 1764 and signed the parish certificate with their mark rather than signatures, indicating that they were both illiterate. Henry died soon after Emma's birth leaving his widow without support. Rather than remain on her own to bring up the child, Mary, née Kidd, returned to live with her own mother in Hawarden in Flintshire. This was to be Emma's home for the next 13 years. Little is known about Emma's childhood circumstances or her family except that they were poor but respectable. Her grandfather, Thomas Kidd, had moved from Madley in Staffordshire to Hawarden where he worked as a collier; it was also said that her grandfather spent some time minding sheep on the Saltney Marshes. Thomas had married Emma's grandmother, Sarah, on 3 November 1735. The family lived in a pretty little thatched glebe cottage, for which

The thatched cottage on the right was Emma's childhood home in Hawarden. It was demolished in the 1890s

Sarah was registered as the tithe tenant, paying £2 a year to Reverend Francis Glynne. Their cottage, with its red sandstone steps, was typical of houses of the area and stood between the Fox and Grapes pub and the chemist's shop, and was pulled down in 1890. Here, Emma was to spend her formative years.

Her mother went to work in a variety of jobs as a seamstress or domestic servant, leaving Emma in the care of her grandmother. With little free schooling as yet available, and girls being largely denied what little there was, Emma's formal education would have been limited, though she may have received some lessons in reading and writing at one of the Sunday Schools that were springing up at this time, or from one of the Welsh Circulating Schools which had been established by the nonconformist Reverend Griffith Jones in 1731. Emma's mother was a tower of strength to her daughter and she was to live with her until her death. She later learnt to read and write, not only in English but also in Italian and French. The only existing portrait of her, now in the Victory Museum at Portsmouth, shows a woman with a plump face, broad nose and small wide-set eyes, lacking

A miniature of Emma's mother, Mrs Cadogan by Norsti

the beauty of her daughter. It depicts her, rather misleadingly, as a dour middle-aged woman when in fact, she was friendly, amenable and most of all could be counted on in a crisis. She was to earn the praise of Sir William Hamilton, Nelson and even the King of Naples who, Emma boasted, called her mother an angel. Nelson wrote of her mother, 'You will remember me most kindly to Mrs Cadogan; I am truly sensible of her worth and attention to our interest at Merton'.[6] Emma seem to have had a brother or half-brother called Charles but the only reference to him is in a letter to Emma from her cousin Thomas Kidd in 1809 informing her that her brother was attending Greenwich Naval College.[7]

Emma's three maternal aunts, Mrs John Moore, Ann Reynolds and Sarah Connor, no doubt rallied round to help. As in many extended families in difficult times, food was shared and clothes handed down. When Emma became successful, she did not forget her relatives and frequently sent them money and helped them to obtain positions, encouraging her cousins to form close relations with both the Nelson and Hamilton families. Although little is known about the Moores and the Reynolds, we do know that Sarah Connor had six children; Cecilia, Sarah and Mary (who would become governess to Emma's daughter Horatia at Merton), Ann and Eliza who married above their station, and according to Emma turned into ungrateful wretches, and Charles whom she helped into a naval cadetship but he eventually went mad; Emma had prophetically mentioned that *there was madness in the family*.[8]

Over the years, Emily grew into an attractive young woman with a heart-shaped face, long auburn hair (with a hint of gold) and blue-grey eyes (one with an unusual brown speck in it). When she was 13, she went to work as a nursemaid for a local physician, John Thomas. The older members of the family may have been responsible for providing Emma with some informal education and were evidently fond of her; the eldest of the Thomas daughters made one of the earliest sketches of Emma still extant. In return, Emma held great affection for them, and would remain in contact with them over the years. At this time, she may also have been inoculated against smallpox, as she never contracted the disease, which preserved her perfect complexion which was later to be much commented upon.

By the time she was 13, Emma had experienced the attractions of London. There is evidence that she was there in on 24 November 1778 to witness the marriage of her aunt Sarah Kidd to Michael Connor, as the marriage certificate bears her signature ('Amey Lions').[9] The city was bustling with people and the streets were full of traders, with everything on offer, from coffeehouses and taverns to operas and the theatre. The author of one pamphlet, *Tricks of the Town*, described the city as a veritable playground; 'London has been justly described as a world by itself, in which we may discover new countries, and surprising singularities, than in all the universe besides.' But a darker side existed to the city, an aspect of which every newly arrived young woman such as Emma should be made aware as one London guidebook of 1776 warned; 'Immediately on their arrival, there are miscreants of both sexes on the watch to seduce the fresh country maiden, with infinite protestations of friendship, service, love and pity, to prostitution.'[10]

London was full of migrants from the country all looking for work. A high turnover of domestics meant that it was easier to find work in the city than in rural areas. People lured to the metropolis were still likely to encounter problems as the blind magistrate John Fielding, half-brother of the novelist Henry Fielding, noted in 1753, ' the body of servants . . . that are chiefly employed . . . are those of a higher nature such as chambermaids, etc whose number far exceeds the places they stand candidates for, and as the chief of these come from the country, they are obliged when out of places to go into lodgings and there subsist on their little savings, till they get places . . . this is one of the grand sources which furnish this town with prostitution.'[11] Emma's sensible mother had probably already secured employment before she left their village. Emma began working as a nursemaid for Dr Richard Budd, a physician at St Bartholomew's Hospital, and his wife Mary at their home at 14 Chatham Place, possibly having been recommended by her former employer. There, she shared chores with her workmate, Jane Powell, a young girl who was destined to become a well-known actress. Emma shared Jane's interest in the theatre and they may both have worked for Thomas Linley the Elder around 1780 at his home in Norfolk Street when he was director of Drury Lane Theatre. Some years later the *Morning Herald* reported, 'Mrs Hart, the celebrated *élève* of Sir William Hamilton K.B., of whose feminine graces and musical accomplishments all Europe resounds, was but a few years back the inferior housemaid of Mrs Linley of Norfolk Street, in the Strand.'[12] Linley the Elder had been appointed director of the Drury Lane Theatre in 1774, and for the next two decades he composed and arranged operas, pastiches, pantomimes, and incidental music for London theatres. Several of his 12 children pursued musical careers and it is believed that Emma nursed his 18-year-old son Sam when he contracted cholera and died. She had apparently become so attached to him and was so upset when he died that she had to leave their service thereafter, though she remained close friends with the Linley family.

Once settled in London, Emily and her mother changed their names – Emily Lyon to Emma Hart and her mother to Mrs

Cadogan, although there is no evidence her mother ever remarried, as has been claimed. Emma concentrated her attentions on earning a living. With few skills and no other financial support, many women had to accept jobs where they found them. Of the many jobs ascribed to Emma – a shop assistant, a parlour maid, a barmaid and an orange girl – most are without foundation. Up until then, Emma had mainly worked in homes of professional families in 'respectable' surroundings. However, in his *Reminiscences*, the fencing instructor Henry Angelo, Hamilton's godson, alluded to Emma also having worked as a maid for an 'Abbess', or bawd, going by the name of Mrs Kelly. This might have been Charlotte Hayes, a well-known madam in Duke Street, St James's, who went under the name of Mrs O'Kelley or Kelly, but there is no reliable evidence for this.

The most famous legend surrounding Emma's early employment was that she was hired by the infamous quack Dr James Graham to pose half-naked veiled in thin gauze as the goddess Hygeia at his 'Temple of Health'. Dr Graham's fashionable establishment was promoted as offering a cure for all ills, a sort of early holistic centre providing an assortment of remedies and nostrums to rejuvenate the body, assist fertility and restore health. Surrounded by classical statues and soothing music, Graham advertised his bizarre inventions and 'medical' experiments, one of which was the Celestial Bed. For £50, a couple could hire it out to sleep on it while an electric current passed through it, supposedly improving their fertility. If Emma did work for him in her early days, it was no doubt due to her love of attention. It is possible she was hired as a singer, since music was part of Graham's repertoire and she had a good voice.

According to the unreliable anonymous *The Memoirs of Lady Hamilton* which came out soon after her death, a naval officer, John Willett Payne, was responsible for Emma's first sexual experience, a result of her attempt to prevent a male relative from being impressed into the navy. Payne was in England in 1779 having just returned from a couple of years on the American station to take up his new appointment as first lieutenant of the *Romney*. He later became acquainted with George, Prince of Wales, and was appointed as the prince's secretary and keeper of the Privy Seal in 1786. It was none other than Captain Jack Payne who, when Emma was 30, brought Caroline of Brunswick to be married to the Prince of Wales in 1795. The liaison between Emma and Payne, if there was one, was brief.

Lured by the attractions of the city's high life, Emma was eager to try and better herself. London was a social whirl of balls, masquerades and concerts for anyone who had the money and the inclination. Libertines, courtesans and those with money would gather at the many society venues to eat, drink and make merry, some coming up from their country estates to enjoy themselves. The huge upsurge in disposable income at this time led to an increase in demand for luxury goods. Jonas Hanway, the great philanthropist, disapprovingly referred to the two decades of the 1760s and 1770s as 'the Age of Pleasure' which promoted a period of licentiousness, vice and corruption, and blamed it for women's downfall. Nothing, he declared, 'tends to pervert the female heart so much as the habit of spending much time and money in amusement and the decoration of their persons, following the example of the superiors in fortune'.[13]

It was this environment of indulgence and opulence that first drew the 16-year-old Emma to the 26-year-old rake Sir Harry Fetherstonhaugh of Uppark in Sussex. Bored with hard work and nursemaiding, Emma desperately wanted to be part of the sparkling life she witnessed. She was fully aware of the sexual power she now wielded and recognised that Sir Harry was the key to the life of pleasure which she coveted. Eton-educated Sir Harry had inherited a fortune and the family's huge estate after his father's death in 1774. Like any educated young man, he had already travelled on the Grand Tour making the requisite visits to Paris, Geneva, Venice, Florence, Rome and Naples to soak up the culture, to see the archaeological ruins and enjoy the arts. His mother looked after his financial interests but Harry was flighty and self-indulgent. A gambler and a flirt, Harry was attracted to young, pretty, illiterate lower-class girls: some years later, at the ripe old age of 71, Fetherstonhaugh would marry his 21-year-old dairymaid Mary Ann Bullock.

Sir Harry Featherstonhaugh

Emma entered his charmed circle and spent the summer of 1781 as Fetherstonhaugh's mistress and houseguest. Uppark was, and still is, a magnificent stately home, with furniture ornately decorated with gold leaf and walls adorned with magnificent tapestries and oil paintings. Situated on the South Downs in extensive grounds, the house commanded a wonderful view all around, and was a welcome relief from the bustle of London. Taking advantage of the countryside, Emma quickly learnt to ride and became a consummate horsewoman, accompanying Sir Harry around his estate. She relished the amusements of high society, enjoying the best food and finest wines at luxurious dinner parties. Emma entertained Sir Harry and his friends with her easy conversation and charm – it was rumoured that she even danced naked on the dining table. Admired by a bevy of rich, handsome young men, Emma fast became the centre of attraction, and revelled in their adoration. The only concession she had to make was to act as mistress to the master of the estate, not a hard

A drawing by George Romney of a theatrical performance at Uppark.
Emma is portrayed on the left next to David Garrick

task for the willing Emma. But in December of that year, her life
was suddenly shattered when she discovered she was pregnant.
Unmoved, and suspecting infidelity, Fetherstonhaugh turned
Emma out.

According to the double standards of the day, women were
supposed to remain virgins until they married, while men's sexual
encounters went largely ignored. Chastity was of the utmost
importance and women who indulged in sexual relationships
outside marriage risked ostracisation from polite society. General
attitudes towards young woman in this position was summed up
by the governors of the Magdelen hospital for 'fallen' women,
who piously opined, 'One false step for ever ruins their fair fame,
blasts the fragrance of virgin innocence, and consigns them to
contempt and disgrace!'. Plenty of girls of Emma's age had found
a charming wealthy man to support them, only to be cast aside to

die in poverty a few years later, or turn to prostitution. Emma's position was now extremely precarious. So far, she had managed to avoid falling into the clutches of a variety of men, or being passed around in libertine circles. She enjoyed herself with a longer affair for a few months. Yet Emma could now see her frivolous life spilling away before her eyes. Luckily, she had already met 32-year-old Charles Francis Greville, possibly at one of Fetherstonhaugh's shooting parties.

Edgware Row

Charles Greville was the second son of the Earl of Warwick and came from a long line of nobility. He lived modestly on a small allowance of £500–£600 a year, with a house in the newly developed Portman Square in London. Primogeniture meant that Greville was not in line to inherit the family estate. There were a number of residual 'noble poor' like Greville in Britain, who were left to pick up small government offices where they could. Many gentry became members of the House of Commons and there was a social mix between upper gentry and nobility who often intermarried. Like many of his circle, Greville was educated at Harrow School and Edinburgh University and took up some of the minor government posts which brought in his small but comfortable living. He held a post at the Board of Trade for six years until he left in 1780 for a job at the Admiralty. Later, he became vice-chamberlain to the King and served in this capacity until 1805.

Greville was not a particularly good-looking man but attractive in his own way. His portrait by Henry Hoppner Mayer of 1810 shows him with a mournful expression with downward-sloping eyes, but an earlier painting by Sir Joshua Reynolds show him as a more attractive character, sitting in the company of the Dilettanti Society, an association formed by the notorious libertine Sir Francis Dashwood around 1733. Initially intended for the entertainment of his friends who had visited Italy, mainly collectors who shared an appreciation of archaeology and art, the society sponsored archaeological trips to sites in Italy and Greece. Its members included Greville's uncle, Sir William Hamilton, the

British envoy to Naples, and the botanist Sir Joseph Banks. Greville had already amassed a vast collection of plants and antiquities by the time he was elected member of the Dilettanti in 1774 and his mineral collection was regarded as one of the finest in England. He had already visited his uncle in Naples in 1769 whilst on his Grand Tour and both men shared an avid interest in archaeology, art and antiquities. Greville was also a fellow of the Royal Society and would later become vice-president of the society and contributed papers to its journal *Philosophical Transactions*.

Emma, by now six months pregnant, turned to Greville for help. He had already expressed concern for her and provided her with envelopes to contact him if she were in need. In panic, she scribbled a hasty note, the misspelling and lack of punctuation making her words appear as if they are pouring out; *believe me I am allmost distracktid I have never hard from Sir H . . . What shall I dow good god what shall I dow I have wrote 7 letters and no anser, I cant come to toun for want of mony I have not a farthing to bless my self with . . . O G what shall I dow What shall I dow.* Emma was in a desperate state but nonetheless pleaded with Greville, *Don't tel my mother what distress I am in, and dow afford me some comfort.*[14] It would seem that Greville already knew her mother.

Greville saw an opportunity for himself in Emma's predicament. Here was a chance to avail himself of a pretty yet cheap mistress, while employing her mother to run his household, affording himself comforts he would not find elsewhere. Sir Harry was a rake and Greville knew his friend would not stand by Emma. To this extent, she was merely following in the footsteps of many poor girls who had gone before her. She put her trust in Greville and hoped that he might take her in and provide for her and her child. After a short period of deliberation, he responded in a long and parsimonious letter in which he pointed out to Emma all of her faults; 'I do not mean to give you uneasiness but comfort, & tell you I will forget your faults & bad conduct to Sir

Romney's sketch of an interior at Charles Greville's house. Emma is seated at the spinning-wheel, a pose later repeated in a portrait

H and myself & will not repent my good humour if I shall find that you have learned by experience to value yourself & endeavour to preserve your Friends by good conduct and affection.' Emma's temper was get her into trouble on numerous occasions but this was the first time it had had any serious consequences. Her outbursts would give Greville much cause for concern, as would her spontaneity – on many occasions she would have to ask Greville to forgive her 'giddiness'. Sir Harry was evidently annoyed enough at her behaviour not to consider helping her and Greville himself weighed up her possibilities. He advised her to make a decision: either to stay with Fetherstonhaugh and learn to please him, although he confessed 'I have never seen a woman clever enough to keep a man who was tired of her',[15] or to leave him, in which case he offered to pick up the pieces. 'If everything fails' he later wrote to her, 'if you mean to have my protection, I must first know that you are clear of every connexion, that you will never take them again without my consent. I shall then be free to dry up the tears of my lovely Emily & to give comfort.'[16] He also agreed to take on her mother as housekeeper and pay for her child's upkeep.

Although grateful that she now had a roof over her head, Emma must have been petrified at the thought of giving birth at a time when many women died in childbirth. Little was known about forceps or the sterilisation of instruments, and less about infection and puerperal fever. Only wealthy patients could afford male practitioners with more knowledge of the new-fangled instruments (mainly because women were not given the opportunities to learn about them), but even they caused many fatalities. Obstructed labour usually entailed the death of the baby and left the mother at much greater risk. Local midwives were still using hooks to pull the baby out in difficult births, often leaving parts of the body behind which left the mother open to infection. Emma was more fortunate in that she could return home and have her grandmother and mother to help her, and where her previous employer and neighbour, the physician John Thomas, was also nearby.

The paternity of the child was never clear. Although the timing points to Fetherstonhaugh, Emma may have already sensed that Sir Harry was becoming bored with her and taken up with Greville, or even a third lover, as insurance against abandonment. It is evident from letters between Emma and Greville during 1782 that she had been to London to see him at least twice before the split with Fetherstonhaugh, and could have well been doing so even earlier, although from his attitude, it is unlikely the child was his. Certainly she appears to have been indiscreet at some stage in her relationship with Sir Harry, for Greville told her, 'Sir H may be informed of the circumstance which may reasonably make him doubt [as to the paternity of the child] & it is not worthwhile to make it a subject of altercation. Its mother will obtain its kindness from me & shall never want.'[17]

It seems Sir Harry had some reason to suspect that the child Emma was carrying was not his.

To give Greville his due, he had most likely saved Emma from a life of destitution and provided her child with a comfortable upbringing, although there was every chance she would have been looked after by her family. In the end, 'Little' Emma was sent to be cared for by her great-grandmother Mrs Kidd, and later by a Mr and Mrs Blackburn in Manchester. Around the spring of 1782, Greville bought a small house and installed Emma and her mother in it. Exceedingly thrifty, he picked a house in Edgware Row in Paddington Green, a leafy street running all the way down to Tyburn, now Marble Arch. The area was still a rural suburb at this time, cheaper than town, and outside the gaiety of London. Here, he could keep Emma away from fashionable society, and maintain the household for under £150 a year and, to further save money, he gave up his house in Portman Square. Emma might visit her dressmaker, take the carriage to sit for the artist George Romney or venture out for some shopping, but most of Emma and her mother's days would be taken up with running the household. This is evident from the detailed and precise accounts she kept, down to the few pence she had given a beggar. Despite her proximity to the London social scene, Emma was to lead the next few years of her life acting as a housewife subject to the whims of her domineering, if charitable, protector.

Although Greville was of noble birth, the household was one of upper middling gentility rather than ostentatious wealth. Not given to luxurious entertaining, he preferred a quiet life. Occasionally he might go to his club, visit other collectors or attend a meeting at one of his societies. At night the couple rarely ventured out; Greville was content to examine his mineral collection while Emma sat and drew, or sang to entertain Greville or occasional guests. Greville held a certain perception of the ideal woman, a popular notion of female gentility based on chasteness and modesty. He saw women as irrational creatures full of contradictions and spontaneous outbursts. He believed Emma needed to be educated (as he believed all women did), in 'reasonable conduct', a game of control he likened to playing a trout and set about educating Emma to shape her into his perfect domesticated companion. According to one popular commentator of the day, John Gregory, whose conduct book, *A Father's Legacy to his Daughter*, was all the rage, modesty was the chief characteristic to which a young woman should aspire, 'One of the chief beauties in a female character is that modest reserve, that retiring delicacy, which avoids the public eye, and is disconcerted even at the gaze of admiration.' Such dictates on behaviour were examples to which Emma was meant to aspire.[18]

Despite Greville's superior air and impersonal attitude towards Emma, he wanted to cultivate her, to teach her to respect herself, as well as become respectable. To his credit, he provided her with music and drawing lessons to keep her amused. Although he attempted to control her youthful spontaneity, complaining to his uncle that she broke out in tempers, he admitted that she was generally sweet-natured. She was also clever and eager to learn, and quickly acquainted herself with art, history and literature. Her generosity was acknowledged by Greville, who exclaimed she would share her

Romney painted more than 50 portraits of Emma

last shilling, or do anyone a good turn; she always looked after her immediate family, sharing her life with her mother, sending money to her grandmother and ensuring little Emma was cared for.

Their recreations sometimes included visiting the parks and pleasure gardens. On one particular evening, Greville took Emma out for an evening at Ranelagh Pleasure Gardens, more respectable than the famous venue at Vauxhall. As they walked round the gardens, Emma, excited by the music, spontaneously burst into song in the midst of all the people and was roundly applauded by the appreciative audience. Although she revelled in the attention, Greville was horrified, hastily bundling her into a carriage and rebuking her all the way home. On arrival at the house, she went directly to her room, changed into her dowdiest dress, and pleaded for his forgiveness. She later related the incident to Romney who recorded it soon after in his portrait of her as *The Seamstress*. The episode was typical of their relationship and an indication of Greville's abhorrence of attention directed at Emma. After this confrontation, she made a series of unsuccessful attempts to control the wilder side of her nature. She earnestly wanted to fit in with Greville's image of perfect womanhood and to act as a devoted and obedient female companion. Meanwhile, he encouraged her to drop all acquaintances of whom he did not approve, leaving her only with homely pursuits. In this submissive manner, Emma was to pass the next few years, living a quiet life in Greville's subdued household.

After the birth of her first child, Emma had begun sitting for the Lancashire-born artist George Romney and they quickly became friends. Both he and Emma came from humble backgrounds and shared a yearning for a better life. Although Romney's father had been a furniture maker and kept a small library which allowed for some sort of education for his son, the lack of formal learning had left him shy in the presence of those with more education. For a time, he worked as a joiner with his father which later enabled him to carve his own frames, make his own violin and design both his studios in Cavendish Square where Emma met him. After a hasty marriage to his already-pregnant wife, he left his family in their home town of Kendal in search of fame and fortune. In between commissions or portraits, Romney had earned his living as a copier of masterpieces but after moving to London his success began to take off. He was introduced to the Grevilles in the early 1770s by his friend the dramatist Richard Cumberland. As a result of the introduction to this aristocratic family, Romney earned one of his first commissions. By the time

he met Emma, Romney was already 47 and had built himself a grand reputation. He first mentioned Emma in his *Diaries* in 1782 when she sat for him in his studio in Cavendish Square, an area then full of sumptuous houses into which the wealthy were moving. For the first of a series of sketches, he depicted her as 'Nature' and went on to paint her in a variety of poses – a Calypso, a Magdalen, a Wood Nymph, a Gypsy, a Bacchante, a Pythian Priestess and a Spinstress; and as Sybil, Ophelia, Saint Cecilia, Medea, Thetis, Ariadne

An engraving of Romney's portrait of Emma as Sensibility

and Miranda. His portraits were based on classical or religious figures – popular representational themes at this time, springing from both the contemporary neo-classical revival and the strong tradition of artists using biblical references. For many years, Romney continued to work on pictures of Emma even after she had left England. In all she sat for him almost 300 times and he made over 50 pictures of her. It was Romney's paintings of her which preserved her image and helped establish her enduring fame.

Romney's muse, a demure Emma portrayed in a white dress

Emma was Romney's muse, stirring him to greater art, and he withered when she left for Italy. His friend, poet William Hayley, admitted to her in a letter, 'You were not only his model but his inspirer and he truly and gratefully said, that he owed a great part of his felicity as a painter to the angelic kindness and intelligence with which you used to animate his diffident and tremulous spirits to the grandest efforts of art.'[19] In turn, Romney, who was over 30 years older than Emma, was a something of a father-figure for her. Her close friendship with Romney continued to grow and some years later, she wrote to him affectionately to remind him of their early days, *You have seen and discoursed with me in my poorer days, you have known me in my poverty and prosperity and I had no occasion to have lived for years in poverty and distress if I had not felt something of virtue in my mind. Oh, my dear friend, for a time I own through distress my virtue was vanquished, but my sense of virtue was not overcome.*[20]

In the summer of 1783, while Greville was away on a trip to Wales with his uncle to inspect the family estates, Emma took her two-and-a-half year old daughter, 'Little Emma', and her mother for a holiday, first to Harwarden to visit Emma's grandmother, old Mrs Kidd, and then on to the seaside at Parkgate. Spas and sea-side resorts were springing up all over England and were seen not only as an excuse to escape London for a break but as places to indulge in a spot of healthy sea bathing. She took lodgings with a sailor's wife and bathed daily in the sea to soothe her urticaria, a skin condition which resembled nettle rash. Worried about Greville's reaction, she kept herself away from other company, even though she was not with him; she wrote to him, *there is a great many Laidys batheing but I have no society with them as it is best not so pray my dearest Greville write soon & tell me what to do as I will do just what you think proper*, adding, *Pray my dear Greville, do lett me come home soon as I am almost broken hearted being from you . . .*[21]

Emma was missing Greville. There had evidently been an argument between them before he left. He was using his extended absence as a punishment for her erratic outbursts and rarely wrote. His silence upset and unnerved her and she implored him, *Pray write my dear Greville directly & send me word how to bile that Bark for parting with you made me so unhappy.*[22] Emma had once again failed to curb her sharp tongue. Acknowledging this, she took the blame for the altercation and attempted to make amends and appease him, with promises to control her temper in the future. Unintentionally, Emma annoyed Greville even further by attempting to foster interest in her daughter; *I say nothing aboutt this guidy wild girl . . . What shall we do with her Greville . . . does not Greville love me, or at least like me . . . is he not a father to my child.*[23] These long descriptions of Little Emma not only bored Greville, but irritated him. He never saw himself as a father and certainly did not want a child around the house. In the end, her attempts to encourage a familial relationship between Greville and the child failed and Emma had no choice but to place Little Emma back with her grandmother. After nine weeks away from Greville, she already sensed he was purposely distancing himself. When they returned to Edgware Row, their life was even quieter than before.

As a single mother, Emma was totally dependent on Greville for protection. Although she no doubt cared for him, it seemed her feelings for him were more in the way of gratitude for saving her from destitution rather than true love. From her letters, she expressed desperation at the threat of being deserted and her main concern appears to be focused on keeping him happy rather than forming any relationship on an equal footing, which in any case Greville would not have allowed. For example, Emma had sent her grandmother five guineas to purchase necessities for the child but in an attack of guilt, thinking Greville would admonish her for her extravagance, she apologised to him and promised to repay him.

The increased affluence of the middle class from the middle of the 18th century had increased the appeal of genteel status which saw a shift towards politeness and a focus on etiquette and manners. The acquisition of elevated social manners identified a person not only with London culture but more importantly differentiated the urbanites from the provincials; it was also a way for lower-class people to advance in society, something Emma was desperate to do. For her, this new cult of manners was a way of rebuilding her reputation and, although she retained her regional accent, she had acquired poise and an increased sense of self-worth. All this was to be threatened as Greville began to grow tired of her. He was starting to see Emma as a drain on his resources and, having kept her for nearly four years, he needed to reconsider his future. Admittedly, he could live sufficiently well on his current income but recognised that he would never achieve a higher standard of living without searching further afield. In order to enjoy a more comfortable life, he needed to find himself a rich wife, who brought with her a substantial dowry and a considerable inheritance. Emma was undeniably an impediment to that pursuit. Furthermore, Greville was now heir to his uncle Sir William Hamilton's estate and the death of Sir William's first wife presented potential problems for him; if his uncle were to remarry and have children, he would no longer be first in line to inherit his uncle's fortune. A letter from Sir William brought home a near miss as his uncle reported the delights of the company of Lady Clarges, a widow with whom he was enjoying a mild flirtation; '. . . had I married Lady C[larges], which might have happened', Sir William pondered, 'it must have been a cruel disappointment to you, after having declared you my heir'.[24] Greville was spurred into action and began to look for ways out of his dilemma – he needed to ensure that his uncle did not find a wife at the same time as ridding himself of Emma. What better way than to bring Emma and Sir William together, thereby disposing of both problems at once?

Greville's uncle, now nearly 53 years old, had returned to England in the spring of 1783 to bury his wife and called in to visit his nephew at Edgware Row and to catch up on family matters. He had charged Greville with looking after his Pembrokeshire estate, and the two had a close relationship. Sir William had gaunt features, a hooked nose and an aristocratic air; he was charming and kind, and proved to be a far more generous man than his nephew. He was a little old-fashioned in his dress and still wore a powdered wig despite their decreasing popularity. Hamilton was born at Park Place near Henley on

13 December 1730. (Although his biographer Fothergill gives this date, the *Oxford Dictionary of National Biography* gives 12 January 1731.) Gossip surrounded the reputation of his mother, as it was alleged she had been the mistress of Frederick, Prince of Wales when Lady of the Bedchamber and Mistress of the Robes to the Princess of Wales, although there is no hard evidence of the affair. Hamilton shared the earlier part of his life and education with Frederick's son, now George III, who referred to Hamilton as his foster brother.

Sir William Hamilton

After leaving school, Hamilton served in the Foot Guards, then as an equerry to the young prince and was promoted to lieutenant. When he was 30, Hamilton was elected to the House of Commons as Member of Parliament for Midhurst in Sussex, a seat he held for the next four years. Although not exactly rich, Hamilton was well-off, with an estate in Wales left to him by his first wife, Catherine Barlow. He had married her for financial reasons but he had developed a sincere fondness for her as she was a devoted companion, and they had shared a quiet life enjoying their musical interests.

As Envoy Extraordinary to the Court of Naples, an ambassadorial post he assumed on 17 November 1764, Hamilton was to live in Italy for the next 37 years. The excavations of Pompeii and Herculaneum, which had lain buried since the volcano Vesuvius had erupted in AD 79, stimulated interest from the whole of the Europe. He admitted to Greville that he was 'mad on volcanoes' and made more than 65 ascents to the crater often taking guests along, including the King and Queen of Naples. As a result of his archaeological pursuits, Hamilton was elected fellow of the Royal Society in 1766, and findings were published in the *Philosophical Transactions* of the Royal Society, on a regular basis over the next 30 years.

At the end of the War of the Spanish Succession in 1714, the Kingdom of Naples, comprising the southern half of the Italian peninsula and including at various times the island of Sicily, became part of the Habsburg Empire. In 1735 the Emperor Charles VI left the kingdom to a collateral line of the Spanish Bourbons. After Emma Hamilton's time in Naples, Napoleon conquered the kingdom in 1806 and made his brother Joseph king. In 1815 King Ferdinand returned and from 1816 onwards styled himself Ferdinand I, King of the Two Sicilies.

An avid collector of art and classical artefacts, one of Hamilton's most important intellectual contributions was his finely illustrated books, *Collection of Engraving from Ancient Vases* (1766) and on his second collection of vases *Collection of Etruscan, Greek and Roman Antiquities from the Cabinet of the Honourable William Hamilton* (1791–5), both in four volumes. In recognition of his work both professional and as a collector, he was made a Knight of the Bath and elected Fellow for the Society of Antiquaries in the same year in 1772. He sold his first collection of vases to the British Museum for £8,400, and it was to form the basis of one of its finest collections. Hamilton was also elected to the Royal Academy of Arts, and Sir Joshua Reynolds praised his books. Hamilton joined the Dilettanti Society in 1777 and confessed his passion for collecting to his nephew Greville: he collected around 350 paintings, 1,000 Greek vases, 600 bronzes, coins, cameos and all sorts of other exotic pieces.

Sir William quickly became enchanted with Emma, calling her 'the fair tea-maker of Edgware Row'. While in London, Greville accompanied him to Christies' auction house, taking in various bookshops in search of art books, and visited the British Museum on business to discuss his collection. Pleased to see his uncle, Greville joined him on a tour of Wales to administer Sir William's estate, followed by a visit to Scotland to see his relations while Emma was in Parkgate. She had become fond of Sir William joking to Greville; *give my dear kind love and compliments to Pliney [sic] and tell him I put you under his care and he must be answerable for you to me wen I see him.*[25] Sir William was nicknamed Pliny the Elder to Greville's Pliny the Younger, the joke connected to Pliny the Younger who had described his escape from the lava descending from the eruption of Vesuvius, and the ensuing death of his uncle from the fumes.

After his uncle had returned to Naples, in an attempt to rid himself of Emma, Greville began feeding him tempting titbits about his mistress's fine qualities, crediting himself with her development. A couple of months later, in March, Greville came to the point, telling Sir William: 'If you did not chuse a wife, I wish the tea-maker of Edgware Road yours . . . In thinking that by placing her within you reach, I render a necessity which would otherwise be heartbreaking tolerable and even comforting'.[26] He informed Sir William that he could no longer afford the expense of Emma but emphasised that she was an exceedingly good companion. Matters became more pressing for Greville as Lord Middleton's second daughter came on to the marriage market and brought with her a substantial dowry. Hamilton was still unconvinced that Greville's plan to hand over Emma would work and needed further convincing. Greville provided further assurances of her suitability as a companion: 'She does not wish of much society, but to retain two or three creditable acquaintances in the neighbourhood, she has avoided appearances of giddiness, and prides herself on the neatness of her person and the good order of her house; these are habit's both comfortable and convenient to me. She has vanity and likes admiration; but she connects it so much with her desire of appearing prudent, that she is more pleas'd with accidental admiration than that of crowds which now distress her. In short, this habit, of three or four years' acquiring, is not a caprice, but is easily to be continued . . .'.[27] Her 'little expenses are trifling' he added, in way of encouragement.

At a time when half of the population of London had gonorrhoea, syphilis or some sort of pubic lice, it was unusual to find a woman with any sort of sexual history who was not infected. Greville was quick to remind his old uncle how lucky he would be to find an obliging woman free from venereal disease, 'At your age a clean & comfortable woman is not superfluous, but I should rather purchase it than acquire it, unless in every respect a proper party offer'd'.[28]

To give him his due, Greville could have turned Emma out as easily as Fetherstonhaugh had and no-one would have given it a second thought. But Greville must have possessed a modicum of compassion for he tried to find Emma and her mother an alternative home. Sir William was already sufficiently entranced with Emma to have ordered a painting of her as a Bacchante before leaving England. But although he found her charming, witty and very beautiful, he was understandably cautious about assuming the responsibility for her. He told Greville, 'I really love her and think better of her than anyone in her situation. But my dear Charles, there is a great difference between her being with you or me, for she really loves you when she could only esteem and suffer me . . . it would never have entered my head to have proposed a freedom beyond an innocent kiss . . . I am not a match for so much youth and beauty.'[29] He even went so far as to offer to make an allowance of £50 a year for her, such was his generous nature. Since the death of his wife, he had settled into a comfortable single life, pottering around Pompeii for artefacts, and was unsure if he needed a woman permanently around.

Finally, Greville urged Sir William to invite Emma to Naples for a trial visit, telling him 'You will be able to have an experiment without any risk.'[30] He requested payment from Sir William, asking him to provide a bond, even sending it back to demand that it be witnessed. It was also up to Sir William to foot the bill for Emma and her mother's travelling expenses which would amount to 30 guineas. Meanwhile, Greville had informed Emma that the situation was only temporary, and that she might return if she did not like it. His intention was that Emma was to suspect nothing more than a holiday break to Naples while he was away on business. Emma was no fool and must have suspected his motives, as Greville half-acknowledged to his uncle; 'She has always said that if ever she was to part she might be weaned by degrees: she talks of the chances of our not meeting again, and that on the least neglect, she will accept your offer . . . '[31] After much hesitation on Sir William's part, he agreed to Greville's suggestion and Emma's fate was decided. With a burst of uncharacteristic insight, Greville prophetically wrote 'Emma's passion is admiration . . . [she] is capable of aspiring to any line which would be celebrated . . . anything grand, masculine or feminine, she could take up . . . '.[32] Emma, having left England in early March, landed in Naples on 26 April 1786, her 21st birthday.

Naples

Emma and her mother set off for Naples accompanied by a distant relation of Sir William's, the 63-year-old Scottish painter and art dealer Gavin Hamilton. He was returning home to Naples after visiting London to arrange his financial affairs and to sell off some of his paintings. Although not greatly recognised in England, he was a well-known collector and artist in Rome during his own time and was to paint Emma's portrait as Sibyl and as Hebe.

The party travelled as far as Geneva where they were met by Sir William's trusted servant Vincenzo, who conducted them the rest of the way. Sir William was excited about the thought of Emma's arrival and admitted to Greville, 'The prospect of possessing so delightful an object under my roof soon certainly causes in me some pleasing sensations'. He knew that looking after Emma would not be an entirely easy prospect as she was upset at parting from Greville. Nonetheless, he was a game old man who took to the task with dignity, promising Greville, 'I will do as well as I can and hobble in and out of this pleasant scrape as decently as I can. You may be assured I will comfort her for the loss of you as well as I am able, but I know from the small specimen during your absence in London, that I shall have at times many tears to wipe from those charming eyes'.[33]

In the 18th century, Naples was the capital of 'the Two Sicilies'. It was the third largest city in Europe after London and Paris, and a leader in archaeology, architecture and the arts. The Bourbon King Charles III had begun the revitalisation of the city in 1734. Treasures and art were imported, old buildings were restored and new palatial royal villas were built, including the commanding Opera House of San Carlo built in 1738 and the Academy of Art in 1752. The residence of the King and Queen of Naples, the Palazzo Reale, was a splendour of luxurious interior rococo decoration, replete with richly embroidered tapestries hanging from the walls, with every door painted in intricate floral designs. Glittering chandeliers lit the huge high-ceilinged rooms and marble statues adorned the niches.

Naples was a city which combined both great luxury and dire poverty, with nobles having to battle their carriages through the filth to reach their palatial villas. The streets were full of prostitutes, pickpockets, fishermen, minstrels, hawkers and ragamuffin children, as Nelson so famously described, 'a country of fiddlers and poets, whores and scoundrels'. The visiting German author Goethe said about Naples, 'the situation and the climate are beyond praise; but they are all resources a foreigner has. Of course, someone with leisure, money, and talent could settle down here and live most handsomely. This is what Sir William Hamilton has done in the evening of his days. The rooms in his villa, which he has furnished in the English taste are charming and the view from the corner room may well be unique. The sea below, Capri opposite, Mount Posillipo to the right, nearby the promenade of Villa Reale, to the left the old building of the Jesuits, in the distance the coast line from Sorrento to cape Minerva probably nothing comparable could be found in the whole of Europe and certainly not in the middle of a great city.'[34] Of the people, he remarked, 'Naples is a paradise. Everyone lives, after his manner, intoxicated with self-forgetfulness'.[35]

In honour of Emma, Sir William would name his Posillipo villa after her. A visitor, Lord Herbert, described 'Villa Emma' as 'the last house a carriage can arrive at', its secluded position not deterring Emma and Sir William from spending time there in the summer. 'It is built on a small rock, and consists of three rooms and a kitchen with a very diminutive fine garden. There are two flights of stairs to come up to it. When the weather is fine a small terrace before the building continues the Setting Room with a large Venetian blind over it to guard it from the heat of the sun.'[36]

To Emma, fresh from winter in London, the smells and sights of Naples must have been magnificent. She had gone from a dull and isolated existence in Paddington to the exciting social whirl and luxury of nobility. Far from secreting Emma away in one of his other residences, as Greville had suggested, Sir William provided her with an apartment in his own home at the Palazzo Sessa which incorporated four richly-furnished rooms for her personal use, which overlooked the unspoilt bay. Sir William took Emma to visit his other residences – the villa to the north at Caserta, and the Villa Angelica, south of the city at Portici near the Royal

Nocturnal Eruption of Vesuvius and the the Bay of Naples by Michael Wucky, 1800. Capodimonte Museum, Naples

Palace and at the foot of Vesuvius. The musicologist Dr Charles Burney who visited Hamilton at the Villa Angelica in 1770, described it as 'situated opposite and within two miles of the foot of Vesuvius, in such a very fertile spot, as every one hereabouts is that is not covered with fresh Lava. He has a large garden, or rather vineyard, with most excellent grapes.'[37]

A new world had suddenly opened up for Emma but on her arrival she was decidedly distraught. She complained to Greville, *I feil more and more unhappy at being seperatted from you, and if my fatal ruin depends on seeing you, I will and <u>must</u> in the end of the summer, for to live without you is impossible. I love you to that degree that at this time their [sic] is not a hardship upon hearth, either of poverty, hunger, cold, death or even to walk barefoot to Scotland to see you, but what I wou'd undergo.* Despite Sir William's kindness and the wonderful sights on offer, Emma remained tearful and unsettled. After only a few weeks, she was already missing Greville, but suspected from the outset that it was doubtful he would come for her regardless of his promises. She tried to remain hopeful and recognised Sir William as a good friend and appreciated his generosity. For his part, Sir William kept Emma busy in an attempt to distract her, and introduced her to his friends and to new interests. He provided her with horses, a fine coach and servants and even Emma could see that he was doing everything to make her happy, as she explained to Greville in one of her many letters to him; *he as never dined out since I came hear & endeed to speake the truth he is never out of my sight, he breakfastes, dines, or supes, & is constantly by me, looking in my face . . . & I am sorry to say it but he loves me now as much as ever he could Lady Bolingbroke, endeed I am sorry I canot make him happy, I can be civil, oblidging, & I do try to make myself as agreeable as I can to him, but I belong to you, Greville & to you onley will I belong.*[38] Meanwhile, she was being pushed to become Sir William's mistress, but she avowed that he could never be more to her than Greville's uncle. With his conscience pricking him, tears sprang to Sir William's eyes when Emma reiterated her faith in Greville since he well knew he had no intention of coming for her. When Sir William guiltily attempted to confess their plans for her, she refused to believe him.

A willingness to accept a bad situation and make it better, even to bend it towards her advantage, was one of the positive attributes of Emma's character. Three months after her arrival in Naples, Emma was taking lessons in music, singing and languages, admittedly initially without much enthusiasm, as she wrote to Greville. Since his early days in Naples, Sir William had been used to entertaining. He was an accomplished violinist and in Naples, he would engage two or three musical servants to accompany him in trios or quartets to entertain his guests. One visitor, Samuel Sharp wrote, 'It is custom when neither the opera nor any particular engagement prevent, to meet at his house, where we amuse ourselves as we are disposed, either at cards, the billiard-table, or his little concert'.[39] The population of the city had now grown to over 350,000, with a constant stream of visitors arriving to see the ancient sites of Pompeii and Herculaneum. The excavations had begun in 1738, and since then, Naples had become the centre of the Grand Tour for all European travellers and Hamilton's residence at the Palazzo Sessa was a particular must for all visitors. In spite of her initial sadness and distress, Emma began to realise her good luck. Hamilton had built a reputation for himself as providing intellectual social soirées with interesting conversation and appreciation of music and art. He encouraged Emma's vivaciousness and lavished attention on her, providing her with trips to the theatre and the opera. He kept a box at the splendid Teatro San Carlo for 77 ducats a year and frequently had opera singers performing for his guests. He was happy for Emma to be seen on his arm at social functions and made it clear to everyone that Emma must be fully accepted. She was now mixing with nobility, as she gleefully reported to

Greville: *I walk in the Villa Reale every night. I have generally two princes, two or 3 nobles, the English minister & the King, with a crowd beyond ous.*[40] Her life was now much more fun.

As an avid collector and follower of archaeological digs, Hamilton was well aware of the need for protection of ancient sites. He admired the work of the director of Antiquities in Naples, Marquis Tanucci, who was overseeing the dig of Pompeii and ordered that any paintings or inscriptions should remain intact where found 'so that travellers will soon have an opportunity of walking in the streets and seeing the houses of the Ancient City'.[41] Sir William had been at the opening of the Temple of Isis just after his arrival at Naples where he had recovered a statue of Venus made of white marble from Pompeii. He remarked to Lord Palmerston in a letter in 1765 that he was delighted that 'all her *tit*-bits such as *bubbies, mons veneris*, etc are double gilt and the gold very well preserved',[42] an indication of Hamilton's appreciation of the sexual in art. Sir William never took matters too seriously, employing his pet monkey Jack to carry a magnifying glass to inspect his antiquities to the amusement of his celebrated guests. On a more serious note, he would send details on his findings to London's Society of Antiquaries. Around 1781, Sir William made the discovery of the worship of the Cult of Priapus which he had uncovered 'in its full vigour, as in the days of the Greeks and Romans' in Isternia and he wrote to his friend Joseph Banks about it. Impotent or infertile Italians would offer up phallic votive offerings at the altar of St Cosmo (the modern day Priapus). His findings led to the publication of yet another book, *An Account of the Remain of the Worship of Priapus* in 1786, considered at the time to be a highly erotic and subversive book, proving that Sir William was not averse to upsetting the moral *status quo*. The publisher was his friend and newly-elected member of the Dilettanti, writer and art collector Richard Payne Knight. Lady Holland wrote, 'Mr Knight wrote a famous work upon the traces

Romney's fascination with his subject continued. Here he painted Emma at a spinning-wheel

still to be found in Italy of a primitive worship. He has assembled a large collection of these symbols in bronzes, marble, etc he is a passionate admirer of the ancients and studies in nature antique forms and contours. Ly. H was his favourite'.[43]

By July 1786, Emma was beginning to perceive the reality of her predicament. She had written 14 letters to Greville and received only one in return. Greville had pressed his case, hinting that she should show more physical affection to Sir William, a notion she rejected; *I was told I was to love, you know how, with Sir W. No, I respect him, but no, never, shall he perhaps live with me for a little wile like you & send me to England, then what am I to do, what is to become of me.* Feeling totally abandoned, she begged Greville to write to her, *to send me one letter if it is onely a farewell . . . Sure I have deserved this for the sake of the love you once had for me.* It is unlikely, in fact, that Greville ever returned her love. The possibility of her returning to England was looking increasingly remote and her resentment towards Greville seethed. She threatened to make her way home under her own efforts, *I shall take my own measures. If I don't hear from you, and that you are coming according to your promise, I shall be in England at Cristmas at farthest.*[44]

Emma was obviously emotionally confused: her letters simultaneously pleaded with Greville, threatened him and regaled him with details of her exciting new life. Although she was missing him, it was obvious she was enjoying her new life which allowed her freedom to express herself, at the same time as indulging in a life of opulent comfort which she had yearned for. Contrarily, despite the bitterness she felt for Greville at his betrayal, she continued to put her faith in him asking him what to do.

Greville finally deigned to respond, giving her the instruction she had dreaded, 'Oblige Sir William' and sending her a blue hat and gloves in way of a final pay-off. Hurt and enraged by Greville's deception, on 1 August 1786, she sat down to write him a diatribe; *I am all madness, Greville, to advise me . . . with cooll indifference to advise me to go to bed with him Sr. W' . . . if I was with you I would murder you & myself boath . . . nothing shall ever do for me but going home to you.*[45] His duplicity hurt her intensely and she quickly fathomed a way of how she might best extract her revenge. Still unsure of the life that lay ahead of her, she was nonetheless quite wisely contemplating how best to make use of the opportunities of a life with Sir William. She realised any influence she held lay in Sir William's attraction for her and warned Greville, *You do not know what power I have hear . . . if you affront me I will make him* [Hamilton] *marry me.*[46] Thus Emma played her best card – although Greville no doubt did not believe her, the threat must have unnerved him. She began to realise exactly how much influence she commanded, continually surrounded by adoring nobility.

Meanwhile, Sir William continued to do his best to make her comfortable and himself agreeable to her. He invited Romney and Hayley, her favourite artists, out to see them. By this time Romney's heavy workload had worn him out and he was too weak to travel. Emma felt even worse than ever at the thought of missing her friend. In the following decade, a series of strokes prevented him from painting altogether. Hamilton had ordered new paintings of Emma for his new apartments, from the Swiss born artist Angelica Kauffmann – one of Emma clad in a Turkish dress, the other in a black rubin hat with a feather that he had given her.

Emma had plenty of other offers from rich young men. She was still young and at the height of her attractiveness. Yet reflecting on past events, she knew she

The Swiss-born painter Angelica Kauffmann (1741–1807) lived in London from 1766 to 1781, where she became a member of the Royal Academy two years after her arrival. She moved to Rome, where her home became a central meeting place for artists and scientists. Her work was typical of the neo-classical taste and interest of the time. She is mainly remembered for her many portraits.

could not rely on the promises of her paramours. After all, she had already encountered two such men who had abandoned her. Her future was uncertain but she realised that if she accepted her position in Italy, she could make herself indispensable to Sir William. She also recognised Hamilton's good qualities and it was obvious to everyone that he doted on her. She, in turn, gradually began to turn her affections towards him.

Emma's Ascendancy

Forced to leave her home in England, Emma had managed to establish a foothold in a new life although she recognised she was still in a precarious position. In Naples, she was surrounded by riches and glamour, and had a chance to mix with royalty as well as to socialise on a scale she had previously only dreamt of. As Emma began to comprehend her situation, she recognised that in order to move forward and secure her position, she must give herself up to Sir William. At the end of December 1786 through the New Year, Hamilton was obliged to leave Emma to accompany the King on one of his hunting parties. As ambassador, Hamilton's job was to keep company with the King and ensure his sympathies lay with England and to encourage his alliance with them against France. Apart from this, his diplomatic duties were undemanding and the only other exertion requested of him was to entertain visiting dignitaries.

King Ferdinand IV of Naples was an uneducated and boorish man. Since his brother had been expected to succeed to the throne, Ferdinand had been given no intellectual stimulation at all in his youth. Both his grandfather and his older brother succumbed to madness and there were fears that he might inherit the congenital insanity. His total lack of interest in ruling his kingdom was more than outweighed by his main passion of hunting and a love of blood sports, often killing hundreds of animals in a shoot. Because of his coarse nature, the King was adored by the *Lazzaroni*, the superstitious Neapolitan peasants, who felt they could identify with him. He frequently kept low company and even called in at the peasants' houses unannounced. Unfortunately, the King's most distinguishing features were his protruding eyes and his bulbous nose for which he was nicknamed *Il Re Nasone*.

King Ferdinand had already been attracted to Emma in the early days of her arrival in Naples; she had claimed *the King [h]as eyes, he [h]as a heart and I have made an impression on it.*[47] According to one visitor, who was later to recall the tale, Emma had an improper introduction to the King. One day out walking in the palace grounds, the King importuned her for a private meeting. Emma insisted she could only consider the request if it was put in writing. She then took the note to the Queen, burst into tears and explained how she had been propositioned by an unknown admirer, asking her what she should do as she handed over the note, knowing full well that the Queen would recognise her husband's handwriting and sort the matter out.

Queen Maria Carolina was the eldest daughter of Maria Theresa of Austria and had been married off to the wayward 17-year-old Ferdinand in early 1768 as a political step to strengthen ties between the countries. The unfortunate 15-year-old Maria Carolina's response was to declare that she might as well be thrown into the sea. Unlike her husband, she grew up to be an educated and intelligent woman, interested in both literature and botany. One visitor to the court of Naples, Lady Anne Miller, described the Queen as a beautiful woman (although this was something of an exaggeration if her portraits and wax bust are true representations of her), with a transparent complexion, glossy chestnut hair brilliant dark blue eyes, an aquiline nose, a small red mouth, even white teeth, and her face with two dimples in her cheeks. Henry Swinburne was more derogatory, deciding 'the Queen has something very disagreeable in her manner of speaking, moving her whole face when she talks and gesticulating violently. Her voice is very hoarse, and her eyes goggle. She has acquired a roundness

Several artists were not kind to the features of Queen Maria Carolina. Landini's portrait of 1785 is an exception. Capodimonte Museum, Naples

in her shoulders and is very fond of showing her hand, which is beautiful.'[48] On the birth of her son in 1777, she was allowed to sit on the Council and, as a result, gained more power, virtually taking over the political role of the monarchy, leaving the King time to indulge in his whoring, drinking and hunting. She overturned some of the ancient laws in an attempt to modernise her country; she updated the old laws, established new places of learning in architecture and agriculture, expanded commerce and abolished old tax laws; she encouraged poets and scientists alike, was supportive of freemasonry despite her staunch Catholicism, and denounced the 'Papal vassalage' in Italy. Madame Le Brun wrote of her in her *Memoirs*, 'She had a fine character and a good deal of wit'.[49] But according to Hamilton's first wife's, her temper ran hot and cold; 'She is quick, clever, insinuating when she pleases, hates and loves violently, but her passions of both kinds pass like the Wind, she is too proud and too humble, there is no dependence on what she says and she is seldom of the same opinion two days, her strongest and most durable passions are ambition and vanity'.[50] She was to bear 17 children during her marriage and retained an admirable stoicism in her duties to them.

Within the whirl of constant entertaining, Emma and Sir William found plenty of time to cement their relationship. It is evident from her letters to Sir William at this stage that the couple had become sexually intimate and Emma had softened towards him. While he was away, she wrote to him, *I was so much in love. I could not be 3 days without sending to you . . . yesterday when you went a whey from me, I thought all my heart and soul was torn from me . . . & think had I the offer of crowns I would refuse them and except you, and dont care if all the world knows it*.[51] The gardener had offered to come and keep her company and play whist, but she joked *but I would rather play at all fours with you . . .* , an obvious sexual innuendo. As a present, she had a likeness made of herself to be fitted in a box for Sir William, *It shall not be two naked, for it would not be so interesting. . . it will be seen a great deal, and those beautys that only you can see shall not be exposed to the common eyes of all, and wile you can ever more see the originals, others may gess at them, for they are saved for all but you,* adding thoughtfully about her breasts, *& I wish they wos better for your sake.* Hamilton took the trouble to write frequently with letters describing his daily hunting activities. In one incident he reported that one of the King's men had their finger bitten off by a wild boar to which she declared seductively *Oh Lord! endead I never will bite your lip nor fingers no more.*[52]

Emma's sexuality has rarely been openly discussed. In an atmosphere of modesty in London in her early days, it was evident that she strove for respectability. Even in the more open licentiousness of Naples, the court feigned to ignore open infidelities. Emma was certainly now in a position to fit in neatly with this position on the surface but her own personal feelings were quite open. She expressed herself sexually with ease, talking with Sir William quite blatantly about having sex with him and how she might please him, even specifying her own preference for 'all fours'. In a world where women were brought up to appear coy, she had obviously shed this mantle quickly, at least privately.

This affair, unlike the one with Greville, grew into a relationship on more equal terms, one where both parties showed each other kindness and genuinely cared for each other. Emma had learnt from her past experiences and knew that as an unmarried mistress, the world to which she had been introduced might be snatched from her at any time, just as it had been twice before. She had learnt to curb her bouts of anger, moderate her demands and to present herself as an attractive a companion as possible in order to retain a place in Sir William's household. She promised Sir William that she had learnt from her past experiences; *now I have my wisdom teeth I will try and be [h]ansome and reasonable.*[53] During a brief period apart, while Sir William was on a trip with the King, she wrote to him declaring, *it is right I shou'd be separated from you sometimes to make me know myself, for I don't know till you are absent how dear you are to me.*[54] Emma could quite easily draw close to someone if they showed her affection.

Sir William kept in close touch with his old friend Sir Joseph Banks, one of his intimate confidantes, to whom he had first revealed his nervousness at the approaching visit by Emma. At first, Hamilton had been fascinated by her beauty, writing to Banks, 'A beautiful plant called *Emma* has been transplanted

The botanist Sir Joseph Banks (1743–1820) accompanied Captain Cook on his first journey to the Pacific in 1768, taking with him at his own expense another botanist and two artists to record their finds. He also played a major role in building the plant collection at Kew Gardens.

from England and at least has not lost its beauty',[55] and then acknowledging to his friend the difficulty of Emma's predicament, 'it is a bad job to come from the nephew to the uncle but she must make the best of it.'[56] As Hamilton came to know Emma better, his attitude to her changed from one of initial physical attraction to one of deep respect and affection. He was constantly impressed with Emma's achievements, and relayed his admiration to Greville, 'Our dear Em goes on quite as I cou'd wish, improves daily & is universally beloved. She is wondefull considering her youth & beauty, & I flatter myself that E. and her mother are happy to be with me, so that I see every wish fulfilled.'[57] She, in return, became his greatest companion, regaling him with gossip from the court and playing hostess to his guests. She knew she had found someone who cared about her, and there was no reason for her not to reciprocate; *My comforter in distress. Then why shall I not love you. Endead I must and ought whilst life is left in me or reason to think on you . . . My heart and eyes fill . . . I owe everything to you, and shall ever with gratitude remember it*[58] and later wrote to Greville, *He is so kind, so good and tender to me that I love him so much that I have not a warm look left for the Neapolitans.*[59]

Nearly a year after Emma had landed in Naples, Philip Hackert, the landscape artist visited them at Caserta in March 1787, and introduced a couple of young men to Emma and Sir William. One was them was the great German writer, the 37-year-old Johann Wolfgang von Goethe. Like many before him, he was initially quite taken with Emma, noting how Sir William had 'after many years of devotion to the arts and the study of nature, found the acme of these delights in the person of an English girl of 20 [she was nearly 22] with a beautiful face and a perfect figure.' The other visitor was his friend, the painter Johann Heinrich Wilhelm Tischbein who had accompanied him from Rome. Tischbein became so enamoured with Naples, he remained there and developed a high regard for Hamilton. He became one of the intimates of Hamilton's circle, illustrated his books and was given the honoured position of director of the Neapolitan Academy of Painting by the King and Queen, so appreciative were they of his talents. Goethe was impressed by Emma's Attitudes; 'The old knight [Hamilton] has made a Greek costume made for her which becomes her extremely. Dressed in this, she lets down her hair and, with a few shawls gives her so much variety to her poses, gestures, expressions, etc. that the spectator can hardly believe his eyes. He sees what thousands of artists would have liked to express realised before him in movements and surprising transformations – standing, kneeling, sitting, reclining, serious, sad, playful, ecstatic, contrite, alluring,

Johann Wolfgang von (from 1782) Goethe (1749–1832), a writer acclaimed as one of the most distinguished representatives of German culture, undertook two famous journeys to Italy, one from 1786 to 1788 and the other in 1790, to escape his tedious duties at the provincial court of the Duke of Saxe-Weimar. He went to Rome, Naples and Sicily to study antiquity and found a like-minded enthusiast in Sir William Hamilton on his way to the remains of Pompeii, which had begun to be excavated in 1748.

threatening, anxious. One pose follows another without a break. She knows how to arrange the fold of her veil to match each mood, and has a hundred ways of turning it into a headdress. The old knight idolises her and is enthusiastic about everything she does. In her he has found all the antiquities, all the profiles of Sicilian coins, even the Apollo Belvedere.'[60]

Back in Naples, Sir William showed Goethe around his collection at the Palazzo Sessa. Amongst all the antique treasures, Goethe came across a strange theatrical set-up. In the corner of one of the rooms, covered in dust, stood an upright chest with the front removed, the interior painted black set inside a splendid gilt frame. It was in this contraption, Hamilton informed him, that Emma had begun assuming her poses, standing within the centre magnificently outlined by the frame. After visiting Pompeii, Emma had begun to include some of the poses of the dancing girls found on the frescoes in the houses as part of her repertoire. They had eventually had to stop this display as it was too difficult to transport the apparatus or to light it properly.

Emma assumes a pose

Emma's 'Attitudes' were a set of poses as classical or biblical figures which she devised to entertain her guests in Naples. They were no doubt influenced by sitting for Romney's paintings and by Greville and Sir William's love of the classics. She may have been inspired by the popular 18th-century parlour game 'pose plastique' to give such performances but her Attitudes were an entirely new phenomena. With no props except for a couple of shawls, Emma captured certain emotions and expressions. Her 'Attitudes' became famous in fashionable circles both in Naples and in England and she would continue to perform them even when she grew older and fatter. They had a dramatic affect on both the Neapolitans as well as the visiting guests; Lady Malmesbury said of Emma, 'You never saw anything so charming as Lady Hamilton's attitudes. The most graceful statutes or pictures do not give you an idea of them. Her dancing the Tarantella is beautiful to a degree'.[61] Emma's pose as the Holy Mother was particularly effective; she boasted to Greville, *its true that the[y] have all got it into their heads I am like the [y] Virgin, and the do come to beg favours of me. Last night their was tow priests came to our house, and Sir William made me put the shawl over my head, and look up, and the priest burst into tears and kist my feet and said, 'God had send me a purpose.'* [62] Her shawls were quite worn out with overuse and she asked Greville to send her some new ones. Never one to bear a grudge, Emma had evidently by this stage, forgiven Greville enough to continue to write to him.

Goethe had initially described Emma as 'a masterpiece of Arch-Artist'[63] but his admiration quickly evaporated. After two months he found her charmless and dull, and her singing inexpressive and 'by no means richly endowed in the mind'. Similarly, the artist Madame Le Brun, who had admired Emma, cooled towards her, deciding she lacked wit and intelligent conversation. Emma was still only 22, a young woman from an impoverished background, trying desperately to adjust to her new environment. Thrust unprepared into a noble circle, other women might have found themselves completely out of their depth but Emma used her natural charm and theatrical ability to win people over. Her lack of education and heavy accent, however, left her wide open to criticism. The snobbish Lady Holland found Emma's rustic inflection jarring, commenting, 'just as she was lying down, with her head reclining upon an Etruscan vase to represent a water-nymph, she exclaimed in her provincial dialect *Don't be afeared Sir Willum I'll not crack your joug*. I turned away disgusted'.[64] Accents were seen as an evident of a lack of breeding. If a person had a particularly strong accent, they were invariably at risk of being mocked.

Others who met Emma were more appreciative of her talents. Lord Bristol, Frederick Augustus Hervey, was enchanted with her and became a firm friend. He had settled in Rome with his wife and youngest daughter, Louisa in 1777, although he was an old school friend of Sir William's, as both had attended Westminster School along with William Cowper and Charles Churchill. Hervey was engaged as chaplain to George III, eventually being made Bishop of Derry. Recognised for his eccentric behaviour, he was to be seen flapping round Caserta in his full bishop's dress.

Emma and Sir William Hamilton's firm and loyal friend, Lord Bristol

Lady Holland remarked, 'Lord Bristol is full of wit and pleasantry. He is a great admirer of Lady Hamilton and conjured Sr W. to allow him to call her *Emma*. That he should admire her beauty and her wonderful attitudes is not singular, but that he should like her society certainly is, as it is impossible to go beyond her in vulgarity and coarseness.'[65] Emma had a soft spot for him and rather liked his lack of ceremony; *He is very fond of me and very kind. He is entertaining and dashes* [curses] *at everything.*[66] Although he was often troubled by gout, he continued to make merry and entertain, and provided both secret information and scandalous gossip to the Queen via Emma.

Emma and Sir William would spend some of their winters in their villa at Caserta in order to be close to the King and Queen who had another magnificent residence there. The Royal Palace at Caserta with its four courtyards was built in 1752 by Charles III, designed by architect Luigi Vanvitelli. On either side of the grand marble staircase were, and still are, niches containing statues. Painting adorn the ceilings and it even contains its own theatre, a replica on a smaller scale of the Teatreo San Carlos in Naples, as well as a library built at Maria Carolina's request; a chapel exists built in the likeness of the one at Royal Palace at Versailles at the request of King Ferdinand. The private apartments of the King and Queen were small richly decorated rooms, their walls and ceilings adorned with allegorical and mythically paintings alluding to the virtues of the King. The first room where Emma sat when in conversation with the Queen was reserved for the most intimate guests of the royals, who were entertained with music, song and poetry. Emma was surrounded by detailed illustrated paintings such as Pietro Fabris's *The Luncheon at the Beach of Posillipo* and *A Party by the Sea shore near Baia* depicting nobility at play, banqueting and dancing. Maria Carolina's own apartments were in *rocaille* style covered in mirrors and stucco of white and gold.

Sir Gilbert Elliot (later Lord Minto), a friend of Sir William's, was a frequent guest. Joining the Caserta household on 27 December 1791, Elliot complained about the poor weather conditions; 'yesterday morning at Caserta it froze hard, from eleven it rained, pouring for twelve hours and in the evening there was an interlude of such lightening you never saw.'[67] Sheet lightning which lit up the sky was common in the rainy season and outdoor leisure activities were curtailed. In winter in the high-ceilinged palaces it was difficult to keep warm, with the wide draughty corridors blasting icy winds through the great rooms despite the huge log fires.

Sir Gilbert Elliot (Lord Minto from 1798), was born in 1751, and was educated in Paris by the philosopher David Hume. He entered Parliament in 1776 as an independent Whig. In 1794, he was appointed governor of Corsica, where he first met and befriended Nelson. From 1799 to 1801 he was envoy-extraordinary to Vienna, and from 1807 to 1813 Governor-General of India. He died in 1814.

As well as ingratiating herself with her noble guests, the locals adored her. Emma was a frequent visitor to the local Convent Santa Romita where even the nuns were enamoured by her. She went to dine with 60 of them but one of them, 29-year-old Beatrice Acquiviva was particularly smitten by Emma; *She kissed my lips, cheeks, and forhead and every moment exclaimed 'Charming fine creature', admired my dress, said I looked like an angel, for I was in clear white dimity and a blue sash . . . She said she had heard I was good to the poor, generous, and nobleminded. 'Now' she says, 'it wou'd be worth wile to live for such a one as you . . . I never met with a freind yet, or ever saw a person I cou'd love till now, and you shall have proofs of my love.'* In turn, she obviously made an impression on Emma, *In short I sat and listened to her, and the tears stood in my eyes, I don't know why; but I loved her at that moment. I thought what a charming wife she wou'd have made, what a mother of a family, what a freind* [sic], *and the first good and amiable whoman I have seen since I came to Naples for to be lost to the world – how cruel!* She gave Emma a satin pocket book she had made herself as a token of remembrance of their friendship. Emma ended her report to Sir William with *I think she flattered me up, but I was pleased.*[68] The British had long had a fascination for nunneries, connected to their antipathy towards the Catholic faith in general. English Protestants thought a woman's place was safe within marriage, not cloistered away in a nunnery.

Emma lost no opportunity to improve herself and began to enjoy her place in Naples society. She learnt French and became fluent in Italian. Her appreciation of art was encouraged under the tutelage of Sir Hamilton and visiting artists. She boasted to Greville that she found *drawing is as easy as ABC.*[69] Sir William already had nine pictures of her and two more being completed, as well as a stone bust, a cameo in a ring, one wax and one clay model. History and dancing lessons were made available to her and increasingly, she took an interest in Sir William's collection of vases learning appreciation of antiquity. Under Galluci's instruction her singing was improving, so much so that by her own admission, one visitor was almost moved to tears by her rendition of some of Handel's songs.[70] Sir William built her a music room and covered the walls in mirrors so she could enjoy the reflected view. She reported to Greville *our house in Caserta is fitting up elegance this year, a room making for my musick and a room fitting for my master as he goes with ous. Sir Wm. says he loves nothing but me, like no person to sing but me and takes delight in all I do and all I say so we are happy.* Sir William often accompanied her on his violin. Emma and Sir William went to Sorrento to visit Duke de Maître for 10 days in summer of 1787. A pretty little town, just a few miles around the coast from Naples, Sorrento could be seen from Naples as an outstretched Peninsula and had become a mecca for 18th-century Grand Tourists. Built on a terrace above the sea, it commands a splendid view for miles around, surrounded by mountainous land. Its focal point was the 15th-century cathedral with marble portals and the wonderful marquetry work of Sorrentine craftsmen topped by an imposing bell tower. While there, they viewed three miles of lava at Vesuvius, where black smoke was belching from it, according to Emma, giving it the *most magnificent appearance in the world*. It was around this time that she climbed to the crater and was fascinated with its fountains of liquid fire, *I was enraptured. I could have stayed all night there, and I have never been in charity with the moon, for it looked so pale and sickly. And the red hot lava served to light up the moon for the light of the moon was nothing to the lava.* While staying at the duke's house, she was asked to informally entertain and sang one of her favourite songs, *Luce Bella*. Beginning with operas and a buffo, she followed up with her classic rendition of a pretty girl with a tambourine; *I sang 15 songs* she boasted to Greville . . . *the finest thing you ever heard, that for ten minutes after I sung it, their was such a claping that I was oblidged to sing it over . . . .I left the people at Sorrento with their heads turned. I left one dying, some crying and some in despair*. Emma perhaps remembered the embarrassment she had caused Greville in her early days at Ranelagh Pleasure Gardens and could now wallow in the attention of others. The locals commended her singing and admired her grasp of their language. One man who was forward enough to suggest her Italian was so good because she must have an Italian lover found himself on the receiving end of a quick rebuff. *I pulled my lip at him to say 'I Pray, do you take me for an Italian whoman that as four or five different men to attend her. Look Sir, I am English. I have one Cavaliere servante and I have brought him with me, pointing to Sir Wm.*[71] Emma gave a dinner to which she invited the famous Italian opera singer, Madame Brigida Banti, yet according to her own account, received a 10-minute ovation for singing herself. She reported to Greville somewhat immodestly that Banti herself declared that she would give anything to have her voice. While on her travels with Sir William, they stayed for nine days with Countess Mahoney at Ischia who was kind and attentive to Emma who, never one to miss an opportunity, again sang for the guests and was even offered £6,000 to sing for three years with the Italian Opera at Madrid.

At her own home at the Palazzo Sessa, Emma was the perfect hostess to the many visitors – everyone was curious about this unknown English woman who had come and conquered Naples and wanted to meet her. Sir Gilbert Elliot, although he thought her manners 'perfectly unpolished', nonetheless, recognised a quality in Emma, referring to her as 'the most extraordinary compound I ever beheld . . . All Nature, and yet all Art'. Despite her rawness and his dishonourable references to her manner and figure, he admitted she had 'excessive good humour'.[72] All received a hospitable welcome no matter what their status. Emma's kindness and unaffected nature made her accessible and likeable, and popular with her guests. She became known as *'una donna rara'* and *'bellissima creatura'*. For all her roughness, Emma had caught the attention of all Naples.

Another friend, Elizabeth Campbell, the Duchess of Argyll, visited the couple with her husband in 1789 and formed a close friendship with Emma. She was tall and elegant, a beautiful women with dark auburn hair and sparkling eyes, who had created a sensation in her youth when she had arrived back in London from Ireland with her mother to make her debut. Over 30 years older than Emma, she was someone she could admire, as well as seek guidance from. When the Duchess died of tuberculosis in 1790, Emma was greatly upset. She confided in Greville, *I never had such a freind as her, and that you will know when I see you, and recount . . . all the acts of kindness she shew'd to me: for they where too good and numerous to describe in a letter. Think then to a heart of gratitude and sensibility what it must suffer. Ma Passienza: io ho molto* [my passion, it was great].[73] Emma was to constantly repeat this refrain throughout her life.

Three years after having been unceremoniously disposed of by Greville, Emma had made a good life for herself with Sir William. She knew she only needed to make a small push to secure her position and ensure a safer future not only for herself but for her mother and child. Moreover, she intended to regain her reputation through marriage. This was to be her first big step in manoeuvring to elevate her status. It was clear that Sir William was not only extremely fond of Emma but thought her worthy of much more than she had been offered in life so far. He was, however, still wary of marriage; he admitted as much to Banks after his friend's tentative enquiries as to the state of their relationship since rumours had reached England that they were in fact already married; 'I assure you that I approve of her so much that if I had been the person that made her first go astray, I wou'd glory in giving her a public reparation, and I would do it openly, for indeed she has infinite merit and no Princess cou'd do the honours of her Place with more care and dignity than she does those of my house; in short she is worthy of anything, and I have and will take care of her in proportion as I feel myself obliged to her'.[74]

Hamilton was well aware that any marriage with Emma might damage his reputation. She was, after all, a woman with a past. He knew Emma was angling for marriage but felt he would not be able to oblige her; he confessed to Greville, 'I fear that her views are beyond what I can bring myself to execute, and that when her hopes in this point are over, she will make herself and me unhappy'.[75] Also, there was the age difference to consider. Hamilton was nearly 60, Emma still only 24. He had already expressed his fear of being cuckolded to Greville and he had every reason to believe that she might not be faithful, given that she had been thrust upon him against her will. Yet Emma was so well-liked and had fitted so well into Naples society that Sir William recognised he had found a potential life-time companion. He had already settled money on her and her mother admitting, 'I give

Emma £200 a year to keep her & her mother in cloths & washing . . . she so long'd for diamonds that having an opportunity of a good bargain . . . I gave her at once £500 worth. She really deserves everything and has gained the love of everybody. . . '.[76] In January 1791, Emma gave a concert and a ball for 400 people to which she dressed simply in plain white satin, without any jewels or make-up. Hamilton called her the 'finest jewel' there, a year later adding 'Take my word that for some years to come the more simply you dress, the more conspicuous will be your beauty, which, according to my idea, is the most perfect I have met with, take it all in all.'[77]

In March 1791, Greville's friend Heneagre Legge and his wife were in Naples and Sir William and Emma called in to visit them to offer their services. Mrs Legge was not well and Emma offered to nurse her but she was unceremoniously rejected on the grounds of her 'former line of life'. Legge made his concerns about Emma and Sir William's relationship quite clear, reporting to Greville, 'Her influence over him exceeds all belief . . . The language of both parties, who always spoke in the plural number – we, us, and ours – stagger'd me at first, but soon made me determined to speak openly to him on the subject, when he assur'd me, what I confess I was most happy to hear, that he was not married; but flung out some hints of doing justice to her good behaviour . . . She gives everyone to understand that he is going to England to solicit the King's consent to marry her . . . that if he should refuse to return on other term, I am confident she will gain her point'. Mortified, he complained, 'his whole thought, happiness and comfort seems to centre' in her presence. Yet even Legge admitted that her talent for entertaining were great, praised her Attitudes as ' beyond description beautiful and striking' but added, although her voice was fine, she did not sing with good taste.[78]

Emma had done what she had threatened to Greville, and was indeed going to marry Sir William. It was not without some reservation on Sir William's part as he admitted to Banks; 'I do not like to try experiments at my time of life. In the way we live we give no Scandal, she with her Mother and I in my apartment, and we have a good Society. What is to be gained on my side?' although he admitted, 'It is very natural for her to wish it, and to try and make people believe the business done, which I suppose has caused the report in England'.[79]

Sir William would have preferred to have continued to live as they were, without any need for nuptials. He was quite content to share his life with her, for her to act as his companion and entertain his guests. At this stage in his life he wanted nothing more than to carry out his duties until retirement with no other considerations to burden him. But he had not counted on Emma's determination to salvage her reputation and her prolonged pressure on Hamilton to make her his wife was enough to make him buckle. He also understood her need for respectability and reckoned, although it might adversely affect his reputation, it was worth it to please her. After some consideration, Hamilton decided it was time to give in, and return to England to marry his 'dear Emma'. They travelled via Rome, escorting Queen Maria Carolina as far as Florence. Greville was obviously concerned as to the moral outrage they might cause when they returned to London and suggested that they should take separate lodgings. Emma wrote back haughtily: *As to our separating houses, we cant do it or why should we, you cant think 2 people that as lived five years with all the domestick Happiness thats possible, can separate.*[80] By now she knew she need not heed Greville, as she wielded the ultimate influence over Sir William's decisions.

Married Life

In April 1791, Emma and Sir William found themselves on their way to England, accompanied by the ever-faithful Mrs Cadogan. On their arrival, Hamilton's first business was to attend court in order to pay his respects to King George III and inform him of his desire to marry Emma. The main concern for Sir William in making Emma his wife was not the fear of gossip but the reaction of King George and Queen Charlotte in England. An adverse response might lead to his being recalled from Naples, something for which the active Sir William was by no means ready. As a representative of the King, Hamilton was obliged to request the King's permission, and although he reluctantly gave it, it was made clear that Emma would not be welcome at court. Although well liked by his subjects, the King was given to an overbearing morality and could at times appear quite sanctimonious. Yet few of the rest of the members of the Royal Family or relatives of George III would escape controversy. In contrast to their rebellious sons, the King and Queen led positively abstemious lives of upright austerity. Queen Charlotte ruled her own drawing-room audiences with an iron rod of decorum and conducted the court ladies in polite forms of entertainment. The highest standards of sexual propriety were demanded, and marital fidelity was expected of all courtiers. It was therefore inevitable that she should refuse Emma the much sought-after entrance to her weekly gatherings.

In contrast to the rebuff at court, they received a warm reception from their friends. Emma's first call was on her old friend

Romney. He was delighted to see her, dressed top-to-toe in a Turkish outfit, accompanied by Sir William. Now frail and depressed, Romney perked up at the sight of Emma and insisted she sit for him over the next couple of months. He painted her

Emma, a detail from a Romney portrait

as Joan of Arc, the Magdalene, a Bacchante, Constance and Cassandra, the first three commissioned by the Prince of Wales. All of London was in a frenzy about her, but it was Romney who recognised her cool head complaining 'all the world following her and talking of her, so that if she has not more good sense, than vanity, her brain must be turned.' He declared her 'superior to all womankind' with 'exquisite taste'.[81]

Despite being excluded from more formal social circles, Emma was enthusiastically received by old friends and family. The Duke of Queensberry ('Old Q'), an acknowledged old rake known for his countless indiscretions with young women, requested she display her Attitudes and singing at his home in Richmond at an evening which he specifically organised for that purpose. The writer and art collector William Beckford invited them to stay at Fonthill. Beckford's mother and Hamilton's mother were cousins and he was a frequent visitor to Italy to visit Hamilton and his first wife so Sir William knew him well. Back in London, Emma was the centre of town gossip, with her every outing the subject of conversation. Everyone praised her theatrical abilities, her singing and her Attitudes. While on a trip with Sir William to see her old friend Jane Powell acting at Drury Lane, they bumped into Gallini, a well-known dance and theatre manager, then running the King's Theatre in the Haymarket. Now in the role of opera impresario Gallini asked to engage Emma promising £2,000 per year, but, as Romney related, 'Sir William replied he had engaged her for life'.[82]

Emma visited her daughter in Manchester for whom Hamilton was now providing £100 a year for her schooling and upkeep. Along with Sir William, she went on a trip to Bath, now a thriving spa town where the fashionable elite gathered to take the waters. Whilst there, the couple met up with Lady Elizabeth Foster, daughter of Hamilton's friend the Bishop of Derry, who reported of Emma, 'I cannot forbear mentioning the impression she made on me. She was introduced to the Duchess of Devonshire by Sir W. Hamilton. She appeared to be a handsome woman, but coarse and vulgar.' She did however,

The eccentric writer William Beckford (1759–1844) personified early romanticism. He supposedly wrote his novel *Vathek*, the Faustian story of a cruel Eastern potentate, in a three-day marathon and in French. A homosexual scandal caused him to flee England in 1794. While abroad he amassed a vast collection of art and books. Upon his return he commissioned James Wyatt to rebuild his family home, Fonthill Abbey in Wiltshire, as a romantic folly. When the huge tower collapsed, Beckford moved on to Bath, where another folly he had built survives to this day.

compliment Emma on her Attitudes 'draped exactly like a Grecian statue her chemise of white Muslim was exactly in that form, her sash in the antique manner, her fine black hair flowing down

her shoulders. It was a Helen, a Cassandra or Andromache . . .'[83]

Back in London, on her wedding morning of 6 September 1791, Emma sat for Romney while he painted her as *The Ambassadress*. He had always been smitten by Emma but by now, Romney was having affairs of his own. Like Emma, he too was to be spurned by the King on account of his private life, being turned down for the job of his portrait painter after Reynolds' death. This was to be the last time Emma would see her favourite artist and old friend. Bidding Romney farewell, Emma and Sir William went to Marylebone

Cosway's drawing of Emma as the Goddess of Health

Church and were married in a quiet ceremony by the Reverend Dr Edward Barry, rector of Elsdon. Sir William's relation Lord Abercorn and Lord Dutens, chaplain to the embassy of Turin, stood as witnesses, with the event reported in *The Gentleman's Magazine*. Horace Walpole wryly remarked, 'So Sir William has actually married his gallery of statues',[84] but his close friends, among them Joseph Banks and the Bishop of Derry, approved of the match. Banks wrote to Hamilton, 'I congratulate you, my old friend, from the bottom of my heart, upon the fortitude you have and the manly part you have taken in braving the world and securing your own happiness and elegant enjoyment in defiance of them'.[85]

Taking leave of their friends and family, they returned to Naples via Paris. At this stage, France was in turmoil, with the Revolution at its height. With the storming of the Bastille on 15 July 1789, the situation became violent and the French Royal Family was in a dire position. After an enforced stay in the Tuilleries, the following year Marie Antoinette and Louis XVI made an abortive attempt to escape and were now held under strict house arrest. As British Ambassador to Naples and his wife, Hamilton and Emma were permitted to visit Marie Antoinette and the Queen was able to pass on a message for Emma to carry to her sister, Queen Maria Carolina of Naples. King Louis was guillotined in January 1793, and Marie Antoinette was to follow her husband at the end of the year.

Horace Walpole's (1717–97) letters are an invaluable source for all historians of his period. The sixth and youngest child of Robert Walpole, the first prime minister in the modern sense and first inhabitant of 10 Downing Street, Horace was at the centre of fashionable society. In 1749 he bought a small house close to the Thames in Twickenham and transformed it into his own 'little Gothic castle'. Strawberry Hill became the setting for his life-long performance, which would today be described as 'camp'. In 1764 Walpole wrote *The Castle of Otranto*, the prototype Gothic novel.

While in Paris, the Hamiltons met up with the Palmerstons. Lord Palmerston (Henry Temple), was an inveterate traveller, a collector of antique sculptures and a member of the Dilettanti Society and Royal Society. He was accompanied by his second wife, a witty, sociable woman with whom he was very much in love. Lady Mary Palmerston wrote to her brother Benjamin Mee about Emma, 'I find her not so beautiful as expected, but certainly extremely handsome and her figure uncommonly fine. She is well-dressed and there is something in her manner very good humoured and a great desire of pleasing . . . She is extremely obliging, without the least appearance of feeling any elevation from the change of her situation. Sir William perfectly idolises her and I do not wonder he is proud of so magnificent a marble, belonging so entirely to himself.'[86] The Palmerstons witnessed the riots in July, and after three months left Paris for Naples, where they would be frequent guests at the Hamiltons.

On her return to Naples, now married, Emma could now be officially presented to the Queen of Naples, not as ambassador's wife but in the same position as any other noble's spouse. Sir William reported to Mary Hamilton, his niece, 'The Queen of Naples, informed of all my proceedings, told me she wou'd see my Wife, tho' she could not acknowledge her as the Wife of the English Minister, & she received her most kindly. Emma very naturally told her the whole story & that all her desire was by her future conduct to shew her gratitude to me, and to prove to the world that a beautiful young Woman, tho' of obscure birth could have noble sentiments and act properly in the great World.'[87] Emma was instantly elevated in Maria Carolina's esteem as she had brought her the last letter from the Queen's sister, Marie Antoinette.

The need for respectability which had been instilled by her mother and grandmother in her youth had stayed with Emma though into her adulthood. Although she may well have shown a devil-may-care attitude to those who disapproved of her unmarried status, there can be no doubt that Emma yearned to become a respectable married woman. The people's approval she sought came from a different rank from those who had surrounded her in her working-class childhood; she was mixing with nobility but had been regarded as an unmarried mistress. It was easier for Sir William to do what he chose – he had after all, been born into nobility and, as both an aristocrat and a man, he could do as he wished without stigma. Emma wanted validation of her position through marriage into the aristocracy. Her plan seemed to have worked as Sir Gilbert Elliot remarked; 'She really behaves as well as possible, & quite wonderfully considering her origins and education. The Queen has received her very kindly as *Lady Hamilton* though not as the English Minister's wife; and I believe all the English mean to be very civil to her, which is quite right.'[88]

Emma had finally found acceptance in the sphere she wanted. The Queen had acknowledged her through a formal introduction, and the rest of the Neapolitan ladies and gentlemen could now follow suit. Revelling in her newly-found popularity, embraced by the Neapolitan Court, Emma described her elevated status to Romney; *I have been received with open arms by all the Neapolitans of booth sexes, by all the foreigners of every distinction. I have been presented to the Queen of Naples by her own desire, she as shewn me all sorts of kind and affectionate attentions; in short I am the happiest woman in the world.* She could not help but wonder if her husband would ever live to regret his actions but knew she would do her best to make him happy. *Sir William is fonder of me every day, and I hope I* [he] *will have no corse to repent of what he* [has] *done, for I feel so grateful to him that I think I shall never be able to make amends for his goodness to me . . . How gratefull now then do I feel to my dear dear husband that has restored peace to my mind, that has given me honors, rank, and what is more, innocence and happiness.* Between 50 and 60 guests came to the embassy every night to be lavishly entertained. British travellers to Naples during 1792 included friends such as Prince Augustus (sixth son of George III), Duke of Sussex, Hamilton's relative William Beckford and Emma's portrait painter Gavin Hamilton. Emma admitted to Romney that learning to control her temper was instrumental in improving her relationship with Sir William and gaining his approval. She joked that Hayley's heroine Serena in *'Triumphs of Temper'*, a didactic poem for young ladies on how to remain good-tempered, had been a regulating influence on her behaviour, *I am affraid if it had not been for the good example Serena taught me, my girdle wou'd have burst.*[89] Sir William was proud of her efforts and aware of the obstacles she had had to overcome as a result of her background. Writing to Horace Walpole on 17 April 1792, he remarked, 'Lady H. who has had also a difficult part to act & has succeeded wonderfully, having gained by having no pretensions, the thorough approbation of all the English ladies. The Queen of Naples, as you may have heard, was very kind to her on our return and treats her like any to her travelling lady of distinction . . . She goes on improving daily . . . She really is a extraordinary being.'[90]

While contentment reigned on the domestic front, civil unrest was increasingly evident on the streets. Elliot reported on the King's reprisal methods which kept his subject subdued; 'the King Of Naples actually loses 6000 subjects every year by assassination, and the wounded are not included . . . Imagine, that eighteen murderers lived in Sir William Hamilton's courtyard last spring till the King obtained leave to take them up, and the battle between them and the sbirri in the yard lasted three hours, in Lady Hamilton's hearing, and they killed two before they could take the rest.'[91] The population consisted of an aristocracy of feudal barons, a middle class of learned people and a superstitious combustible peasant class made up mainly of fishermen and porcelain makers, capable of open rioting at any time. Mob rule had already overtaken France and Maria Carolina was in fear that this would happen in her own country.

It was also becoming apparent that hostilities would inevitably come to Naples, war having broken out between France and Austria and Prussia, although Hamilton had concentrated his efforts on keeping Naples out of the conflict. Maria Carolina was already strongly aligned to the English but officially at least, adhered to the line of neutrality in order to keep peace. Hamilton effectively divided the Neapolitan court from that of the other Bourbons. He wrote to Lord Weymouth, 'it is the Queen of Naples that actually governs this country' and she was most definitely on the side of the British.[92] Much to her annoyance, the court of Naples was obliged to receive the French envoy Monsieur Mackau in August 1792. They treated him cordially but coolly and were still most anxious about the plight of the French Royal Family who were now under house arrest. Mackau provoked further hostility by appearing in his National Guard uniform.

At the end of the year, Hamilton fell seriously ill, giving Emma a chance to prove her devotion. She nursed him through the worst, sitting by his bedside for eight days and nights. After his recovery, she considered her potential loss, musing to Greville; *Endead I was almost distracted from such extreme happiness at once to such misery . . . What could console me for the loss of such a husband, friend and protector? For surely no happiness is like ours.* Despite her concerns for Hamilton, Emma did not forget her obligations to her grandmother. With Hamilton ill, she could not ask him for money, so she turned to Greville; *You must know I send my grandmother every Christmas twenty pounds, and so I ought, I have 2 hundred a year for nonsense, and it wou'd be hard I cou'd not give her twenty pounds when she has so often given me her last shilling. As Sir Wm is ill I cannot ask him for the order but if you will get the twenty pound & send it to her you will do me the greatest favour.* She was concerned that her grandmother should not think she had forgotten her, *& I wou'd not keep her poor old heart in suspense for the world.* She even felt guilty about the amount of money she spent on clothes; *The fourth of November last I had a dress on that cost twenty-five pounds, as it was Gala at Court; and believe me I felt unhappy all the while I had it on.*[93]

While Queen Maria Carolina directed her main attention to ruling her country, she remained relatively unconcerned about her husband's extra-marital affairs and she herself had reputedly taken other lovers, one of them rumoured to have been her close advisor and minister Sir John Acton. Much esteemed by Hamilton who regarded him as 'a very sensible man, and has the character of an excellent Sea Officer',[94] it was Acton who would help to guide

Sir John Acton (1736–1811) was a statesman working for the King of Naples. His duties started in 1778 and he soon became the favourite of Queen Maria Carolina. His tyranny is blamed for the insurrection of 1798. His official role in Naples only ended when Napoleon conquered the Kingdom. Sir John died in Palermo five years later. His grandson, the historian Lord Acton (John Acton, 1834–1902, baron 1869), who was born in Naples, famously said in 1887 that 'power tends to corrupt and absolute power corrupts absolutely'.

them through the oncoming troubles. Acton admired Emma and declared her 'a worthy and charming young lady.'[95]

Emma and Sir William's lives were becoming more closely intertwined with those of the Neapolitan Royal Family. The Queen was nearly 40 when she met Emma and took an immediate liking to her. Emma, in turn, was to devote much of her time to the Queen – both would benefit from the friendship. Maria Carolina, with her political acumen, saw that Emma, as wife of the British Ambassador, would serve a useful purpose as a persuasive intermediary between her and Britain. Emma, although not exactly politically savvy, was wily enough to see an opportunity of furthering her position at Court. They also became genuinely fond of each other.

An unexpected and unwelcome French fleet arrived at Naples in January 1793, and insulted the King and Queen still further when a feast was held on board with toasts to liberty and revolution. France had already declared war on Austria in April of the previous year, so Maria Carolina was hardly unbiased against them. An alliance to fight against the French had been formed in 1792 by Prussia and Austria. After the execution of Louis XVI, Britain joined the alliance fighting revolutionary France in January the following year which combined the forces of Spain, Netherlands, Austria, Prussia, England, Naples and Sardinia-Piedmont. Although Naples was still supposed to be neutral, Maria Carolina took action against those she saw as her enemies: she expelled Citizen Mackau, the French Jacobin representative at Court, and sent out her fleet to engage the French. Hamilton wrote to the Foreign Secretary Lord Grenville with his appraisal of the situation; although the Neapolitans abhorred the French, the populace were now becoming aware of their potential power seeing the French revolutionaries as their example; 'They are now sensible that in this country justice does not exist. That the government of it is very defective, and that the people have a right not to be trampled on.'[96] He realised that Ferdinand had no concern for politics and government was left to the harsh tactics of the Queen. She knew there were spies in their midst and attempted to stem the rising rebellion, taking a tough line – she instructed the people of Naples to send their French servants home, made any gathering of more than ten people illegal, and jailed any Jacobin sympathisers.

Emma now felt secure enough to start letting herself go a little. Even though generally she was carrying herself well, she was not averse to a little vulgarity, something which her husband apparently encouraged. Visiting in March 1793, Lady Palmerston remarked; 'Lady H is to me very surprising, for considering the situation she was in she behaves wonderfully well', adding, ' Now and then to be sure a little vulgarness pops out, but I think it's more Sir William's fault, who loves a good joke and leads her to enter into his stories, which are not of the best kind'.[97] With such an avalanche of contemporary comment, it cannot be doubted that Emma was no longer maintaining the stifling decorous attitude that Greville had insisted on. She was becoming more boisterous and allowing the bawdier side of her personality to show. Never one to be affected, who could blame her for telling racy stories and behaving as she liked?

By June 1793, Naples had become so volatile that the Hamiltons, along with the Royal Family decided to move out of the city temporarily. *For political reasons we have lived eight months at Caserta*, she informed Greville, *that is, making this our constant residence & going twice a week to town to give dinners, balls etc and returning here at 2 or 3 o'clock in the morning.* Emma would spend three hours most evenings talking privately with the Queen *tête-a-tête*. She kept a level head and refused to be trapped by affectations, and was more the liked for it by the ministers' wives. She continued, *I had been with the Queen the night before alone* en famille *laughing and singing etc. but at the drawing room I kept my distance, and pay'd the Queen as much respect as tho' I have never seen her before, which pleased her very much*. Despite Emma's description of the Queen, she must have felt wretched with worry. Her sister was in detention at the Temple in Paris, dressed in black mourning after the murder of her husband, spending her last lonely days listening to the crowds who gathered below her window to sing hostile songs about her.

Emma's letters to Greville were frequently filled with domestic details: every day, the Hamiltons accompanied the King and Queen for a walk in the early morning fresh air round the English Garden in the grounds of the Royal Palace at Caserta; *Sir W. & me are there every morning at seven o'clock, sometimes dine there & allways drink tea*. Emma, along with Sir William, had taken up studying botany *not to make ourselves pedantical prigs to shew our learning like some of our travelling neighbours, but for our own pleasure*;[98] Sir William had caught the diarrhoea doing its rounds of Naples; the Plymouths visited; Emma asked him to send her items she could not find in Naples, *some Ribbands & fourteen yard of fine muslin work'd for a gown or fine leno* and requested a new riding hat. Her relationship with Sir William was now close and she was only too happy to emphasise the fact; *Sir William told me he loved me better than ever & had never for one moment repented.*[99] She hinted at the sexual side of their life, *We live more like lovers than husband and wife . . .,*[100] and perhaps to pique Greville further, in remembrance of their own continual arguing, remarked pointedly, *My dear sir William is very well & as fond of me as ever . . . you wou'd be delighted to see how happy we are, no quarrelling, nor crossness nor caprices, all nonsense is at an end . . .* Emma also expressed concern for her first child who would now be nearly 13; *Do send me a plan how I could situate Little Emma, poor thing; for I wish it.*[101]

Hamilton, in the autumn of his years, when he could have been expecting a quiet life running up to his retirement, began for the first time to actively participate in full diplomatic negotiations. The war finally reached Naples when Captain Horatio Nelson arrived on 10 September 1793. This meeting was to change all of their lives forever.

Enter Nelson

Nelson's arrival was a significant event for both naval policy and the Hamiltons. France had declared war on Britain in February 1793, and as a result, there was a pressing need for a British presence to protect the area from the French. The British had gained a foothold in the Mediterranean after Admiral Hood had occupied Toulon the previous month, and reinforcements were urgently needed to hold the port. Nelson sailed into Naples aboard HMS *Agamemnon* on 10 September under orders to recruit troops from Turin and Naples to help maintain the British occupation of Toulon.

In August 1793, the main French Mediterranean naval base of Toulon was the scene of a royalist uprising against the new revolutionary government. Seizing control of the city, the rebels handed it over to the British Mediterranean fleet commanded by Admiral Lord Hood. Captain Nelson was sent in the *Agamemnon* to Naples for troops to help in the occupation of this vital strategic prize. The Revolutionaries laid siege to the city, their artillery being commanded by one Napoleon Bonaparte, and the British were eventually forced to withdraw in December.

Despite Naples' supposed neutrality, Hamilton and Acton, the Queen's minister, had negotiated a secret treaty with Britain in July that year, forming an Anglo-Neapolitan alliance. The agreement was that the Neapolitans would have the protection of the British navy and halt any trade with France. In return, Naples would remain technically neutral but supply troops, ships and frigates. Nelson therefore expected assistance from the

Neapolitans, and received it. Hailed as the saviour of Italy, he was immediately offered 6,000 troops while his fatigued and undernourished crew were fed and made comfortable; 'My poor fellows have not had a morsel of fresh meat or vegetables for near nineteen weeks', Nelson complained to his wife, 'and in that time I have only had my foot twice on the shore of Cadiz.'[102] Prior to this expedition he had been laid up on half-pay in Norfolk, his living expenses buttressed by the interest on the dowry of £4,000 his wife's uncle had given them. Bored at home, when war broke out between France and Britain, Nelson was only too eager to return to sea.

Nelson was born 29 September 1758 at Burnham Thorpe, Norfolk. His family lived for many years at the rectory where his religious upbringing held with him for the rest of his life – nearly all his letters carry the lines 'God Bless' or 'Trust in God'. His mother's death when he was nine years old, no doubt helped mould his determined character. He had seven surviving siblings from the 10 children his mother had borne over 17 years. With little money to spare, when he was 12 Nelson was taken to sea by his uncle Maurice Suckling, a captain in the Royal Navy. Nelson served in a variety of ships, and rose quickly in rank, becoming a post captain three months short of his 21st birthday in 1779.

Nelson's family were an important part of his life and he remained close to them. Maurice, his eldest brother, was a bachelor employed as a Navy Office clerk. William, next in age, was a Cambridge graduate who became a rector at Hilborough, Norfolk on £700 a year, and had an avid lust for self-promotion. He married Sarah Yonge and they had two children, Horace and Charlotte, who would both later be looked after by Emma and Nelson. His two younger brothers, Edmund and Suckling, died while in their twenties and thirties. His sister Susannah married Thomas Bolton, an unsuccessful trader in Norwich, who

A portrait of the young midshipman Horatio Nelson at 19

later tried his hand as a farmer in Cranwich, Norfolk; Thomas borrowed money from both Fanny and Emma, gambling much of it away. Nelson's favourite sister Kitty married George Matcham, explorer and employee of the East India Company and they had at least eight children.

Prior to meeting his wife, Nelson had liaisons with other women. One was the 16-year-old Mary Simpson at Quebec in 1782; at St Omer he met with the La Mourie sisters; in 1784, still in France, he wooed a Miss Andrews; and he even fell in love with a married women, Mrs Moutray in the Leeward Islands. At 28, he eventually married Frances Nisbet in a small church at on the island of Nevis with Prince William, the King's son, as best man. She was a widower and had a son Josiah from her previous marriage. Nelson was not in love with her but did admire her mind; he thought her mental accomplishments as 'superior to most people of either sex', although in reality, these were not great. He was not faithful to Fanny and she alone was never enough for Nelson. He had women in his cabin while away from her as seen in the diary entry of Captain Thomas Fremantle for 3 December 1794 – 'Dined at Nelson's and his dolly'; and in August 1795 'Dined with Nelson. Dolly aboard who had a sort of abscess in her side, he makes himself ridiculous with that woman';[103] and again in September, 'Dolly' being the opera singer Signora Adelaide Correglia of Leghorn. Although slight in stature (just under 5ft 6in in height), Nelson was brave and headstrong, an idealist who put his love of his country above all else. His magnetism and ability to capture the hearts of his men meant he could rely on them to follow when he led them into battle. His approach to life was exemplified by a saying in a letter to Emma, 'The Boldest measures are the Safest'.[104]

Nelson was nearly 35 when he first met the 28-year-old Emma on his arrival at the British Embassy the day after his landing in Naples Bay. Although Nelson was on shore for only four days, the first meeting between himself, Emma and Sir William must have had a great effect on all of them as they were to keep up a correspondence thereafter. Nelson and Hamilton liked and trusted each other immediately. Sir William told Emma, 'The captain I am about to introduce to you is a little man and far from handsome but he will live to be a great man',[105] and he instinctively took Nelson as his friend. Nelson had been greatly fatigued but once he had recuperated, the Hamiltons took him to dine at court and to concerts, and introduced him to their English friends, with his days taken up in discussion with Hamilton, Acton and the King. In return for all their hospitality, Nelson invited them to dine on board ship with Sir William and Emma providing all the food and cutlery. They went on board that morning along with other nobles, awaiting the arrival of the Royal Family who were expected at one o'clock, the ship festooned in flowers and bunting. Suddenly a message was received that a French ship had been sighted and the guests were hastily sent ashore so Nelson could give chase.

In his haste, Nelson had inadvertently taken their butter-pan with him; he sent a note apologising, 'Don't call me an ungrateful guest for it for I assure you I have the highest sense of your and Lady Hamilton's kindness, and shall rejoice in an opportunity of returning it.'[106] He wrote to his wife about the meeting with Emma, praising her for taking Josiah, his step-son whom he had brought along as his midshipman, under her wing and showing him around Naples. Nelson wrote to his wife, 'Lady Hamilton has been wonderfully kind and good to Josiah. She is a young woman of amiable manners, and does honour to the station to which she is raised.'[107] Emma and Nelson would not meet again until Nelson's return five years later.

Between June and August 1794, Mount Vesuvius erupted in a violent display which shook the whole of the area, destroying the nearby town of Torre del Greco. At least 18 deaths resulted from the eruption. The eruption was the biggest Emma had ever seen. Billowing clouds of back smoke covered the whole of the mountain emitting flashes during day into night, and buildings were collapsing under the weight of the ash. The religious population reacted by mounting processions carrying the phial of the dried blood of their beloved saint followed by the saint's golden statue. Hamilton took a trip on his boat to examine the state of the sea and observed that it was scalding hot and boiling as in a cauldron. He and his boatman only narrowly escaped as his boat began to come apart in the heat and they hurriedly rowed to the relative safety of the shore. To the concern of Emma, he then proceeded to climb the still-active crater.

The pair received visits from their old friends, the Bishop of Derry and the young Prince Augustus, and arranged a concert at which Mrs Elizabeth Billington was engaged to sing. In way of appreciation, the eccentric prince attempted to join in, warbling along with the songstress. Unfortunately, he was tone deaf and the bishop was aghast at the noise; 'Pray cease', he pleaded, 'you have the ears of an ass.'[108] It is unsurprising that Emma admired the London-born Mrs Billington; she was the same age as Emma, and had been a child prodigy, having composed and published various sonatas before she was 13. Taught by J C Bach, she played the piano, had a sweet voice and a considerable knowledge of music. Mrs Billington made her Naples debut at the Hamilton's palace and so excited the King and Queen that they arranged for her to sing at the San Carlo Opera House.

Emma had come to adore the Queen and was now her close confidante. In 1794, she boasted to Greville, *She is everything one can wish – the best mother, wife, and freind in the world. I live constantly with her, and have done intimately so for 2 years, and I never have in all that time seen anything but goodness and sincerity in her.* So close had they become that rumours began circulating that Maria Carolina and Emma were conducting a lesbian relationship. Emma wrote

Maria Carolina

to Greville to complain about certain lewd books which were spreading tales about the Queen, instructing him not to believe any gossip he heard; . . . *if you ever hear any lyes about her contradick them & if you shou'd see a cursed book written by a vile French dog with her character in it don't believe one word . . . if I was her daughter she cou'd not be kinder to me & I love her with all my soul . . .*[109] The spreading of such tales was a political tactic similar to that used during the French Revolution when pornographic leaflets were distributed throughout Paris accusing Marie Antoinette of having affairs with her ladies-in-waiting.

Emma was now putting on weight as a result of too much good food and wine. On his visit in 1795, Sir Gilbert Elliot, previously most complimentary of Emma, unkindly remarked 'Her person is nothing short of monstrous for its enormity, and is growing every day. She tries hard to think size advantageous, but is not easy about it', but nonetheless admired her beauty and 'considerable natural understanding'.[110] A couple of months later, Sir William eventually fell ill again to the bilious fevers which were plaguing him. Emma received a note from the Queen expressing her concern for him, advising Emma to 'put confidence in God who never forsakes those who trust in Him . . .', while confirming her 'sincere friendship'.[111] Hamilton was in bed for eight days with Emma carefully nursing him, never leaving his side. Emma confirmed, *My ever dear Queen as been like a mother to me since Sir William as been ill: she writes to me four or five times a day, and offered to come and assist me; <u>this is friendship.</u>*[112]

The Queen was attempting make friends with the English in Naples. Taking political matters in hand, she ignored Ferdinand and handed over whatever political information she thought might be useful to Emma to give to Sir William, while supporting Acton's close affiliations with him. With the Queen's encouragement, Emma began to play a diplomatic role in Naples, although this has been frequently been played down. The most important opening into the world of spying for Emma came with the discovery of secret letters sent to King Ferdinand between 1795 and 1796. Charles of Spain, Ferdinand's brother, was urging him to fall in with France just as Spain was planning to do. Unbeknown to the King, these letters were 'borrowed' by the Queen and given to Emma to make copies. She also sent Emma confidential papers 'which may be used by your husband'.[113] These were then hastily couriered to London to inform the government of the latest political developments. Emma reported to Greville in 19 April 1795, *against my will, <u>owing to my situation here</u> I am got into politicks, and I wish to have news for my dear beloved Queen whom I adore nor can I live without her, for she is to me a mother, friend & everything . . . she is the first woman in the world, her talents are superior to every woman in the world and her heart is the most excellent and strictly good and upright.*[114]

Emma recognised the opportunity to increase her importance. She had won the trust of the Queen who was now inviting her to play a vital role relaying clandestine messages. Her sense of drama might well be responsible for her overstating her contribution in the whole scheme of events but there is plenty of evidence which points to Emma playing a useful diplomatic role – she knew she could assist her government and did what was expected of her. In an attempt to gain a pension some years later, she claimed that her influence with the Queen was instrumental in obtaining information for the British government as to the shifting alliances of Spain towards France, and its declaration of war against England on 11 October; *By unceasing cultivation of this influence* [with the Queen] *and no less watchfullness to turn it to my country's good, it happened that I discovered a courier had brought the King of Naples a private letter from the King Of Spain. I prevailed on the Queen to take it from his pocket unseen. We found it to contain the King of Spain's resolution to withdraw from the Coalition, and join the French against England. My husband at this time lay dangerously ill. I prevailed on the Queen to allow my taking a copy, with which I immediately dispatch'd a messenger to Lord Grenville, taking all the necessary precautions; for his safe arrival then became very difficult, and altogether cost me about £400 paid out of my privy purse.*[115] The British government would have been aware of this political wavering and Emma was overstating her case in the hope of a pension, manipulating history to portray herself as a heroine. The Queen would have communicated the information to Hamilton in any case in order to ensure the continued protection of her British allies as all her hopes now lay with the Royal Navy. But there can be little doubt that Emma oiled the wheels of the machinations, and certainly was to bring to bear all her fortitude in assisting the Royal Family when the situation worsened. Her quick wits and fluency in French and Italian were also extremely useful.

Emma wrote to the diplomat Lord George Macartney in February 1796 regarding the Royal manoeuvrings; the King was having some difficulty in deciding what to do, or who to side with, the Queen prevailing upon him to thrown his allegiance behind the British. Emma reported, *I have this moment received a letter from my adorable Queen. She is arrived with the King. She has much to do to persuade him ; but he approves of all <u>our prospects</u>. She is worn out with fatigue. Tomorrow I will send you her letter.*[116] Hamilton confirmed that Emma's influence over the Queen had grown considerably as had her relationship with him; 'Here we are as usual for the hunting and shooting season, and Emma is not at all displeased to retire with me at times from the great world. The

Queen of Naples seems to have great pleasure in her society. She sends for her generally three or four times a week . . . in fact all goes well *chez nous*'.[117]

Private matters re-emerged with Greville's queries as to the future of Emma's 14-year-old daughter. He suggested she might be put into some trade or other but wanted Emma's agreement or alternative suggestions. He had already passed over the financial burden of her to Hamilton four and a half years earlier, with a studied objectivity; 'The natural attachment to a deserted orphan may be supposed to increase from the length of time she has been protected,' he wrote to Sir William, assuring him 'I have avoided any such sentiment . . . ' and promptly passed on the accounts for her support.[118] Little Emma was a reserved girl, not very attractive, with large eyes and 'a sensible look'. Greville feigned not to know about her background telling Hamilton 'I am still uncertain of her history but I believe her to be niece to Mrs C., [Cadogan] & that her parents are alive; this she should know, for her age is now such as to make it proper to give her at least the comfort of knowing, or the certainty that she cannot be the better from receiving the information, neither of which I am able to give, unless Ly H. will inform you, or communicate to me her wishes.'[119] It would appear that both Emma and Greville had kept the truth from Sir William.

Political Unrest

The situation in Naples was now deteriorating, with the constant fear of invasion hanging over the city. One by one, Britain's allies had fallen by the wayside: Holland had fallen to France in 1794; Austria and Prussia were defeated at battles at Wattignies and Weissenbourg respectively and both were forced to make peace with the French in 1795; the Netherlands and Spain were to join them by the following year. During 1796, Bonaparte took over the French army in Italy, entered Milan and defeated Austria and Sardinia. In order to keep the peace, Naples had to come to terms with France: no more than four anti-French ships were allowed at a time into the bay and all imprisoned Frenchmen were to be released.

Emma, Sir William and the Royal Family were in the thick of the political unrest. Sir William had become increasingly concerned as to the safety of Naples conveying his fears to Greville, 'I must own to you that I think Italy is in great danger of being completely plunder'd and ruin'd unless some unforeseen accident shou'd operate in her favour, and that very soon . . . What a pity that Italy shou'd be robbed of its finest marbles, pictures & bronzes . . .',[120] somewhat ironic, given his own record for acquiring Italian antiquities. Feeling excited about being in the middle of a drama, Emma relayed the intrigues in which she was involved,; *We have not time to write to you*, she apologised to Greville, *as we have been 3 days and nights writing to send by this courier letters of consequence for our government. They ought to be grateful to Sir William & <u>myself in particular</u>, as my situation at this Court is <u>very extraordinary</u>, & what no person as yet arrived at; but one as no* *thanks, & I allmost sick of grandeur. We are tired to death with anxiety, and God knows where we shall soon be, and what will become of us, if things go on as they do now.*[121] Despite her denials, Emma was enjoying being in the middle of a tragedy where she could play a major role. Her high sense of the dramatic could be played out for real but she was possibly unaware of the very real threat from the mob.

Both Hamilton and Acton knew that in reality the treaty between Naples and France was worthless and that France intended to invade whenever convenient. As the French were attacking British ships in the Mediterranean, Britain began withdraw from the region. Nelson, annoyed at the withdrawl of British support, complained bitterly to the Hamiltons in October, 'Till this time, it has been usually for the allies of England to fall from her, but till now she never was known to desert her friends while she had the power of supporting them.'[122] Meanwhile Maria Carolina despaired; spies were everywhere and capital sentences were being handed out; all the prisons were full of traitors and bloody massacres were occurring in the streets. The Royal Family demanded contributions from the monied Neapolitans as they gave their own jewels and money to finance the war against the French. The Queen asked Emma to tell the British, 'God save great George our King' and declared she loved the British prince as she did her own son.[123]

News of Nelson's victory at the Battle of Cape St Vincent on 14 February 1797 encouraged

On 14 February 1797, a British fleet of 15 battleships under Admiral Sir John Jervis (later Lord St Vincent) defeated a Spanish fleet of 25 sail-of-the-line at the Battle of Cape St Vincent. In this battle, Nelson (commanding HMS *Captain*) took his ship out of the line to intercept a Spanish counter-attack, boarded and captured the 80-gun *San Nicolas* and then crossed from that ship on to the even-larger *San José* and capturing it in turn, a feat dubbed 'Nelson's Patent Bridge for Boarding First Rates'. It was this action that first made Nelson a national hero.

his friends back in Naples. While Nelson was at sea, Hamilton did his best to keep him up to date with regular dispatches while Emma filled him in on political intrigues. Hamilton wrote congratulating him, 'Lady Hamilton and I admire your constancy, and hope the severe service you have undergone will be handsomely rewarded.'[124] Maria Carolina now felt confident enough to reverse some of her harsh policies; she dismissed the Inquisitor of State and, cheered on by the *lazzaroni*, released all her captives, something which Emma did not entirely approve of. She complained to Nelson, *these pretty gentlemen that had planned the death of their Majesties are to be let out in society again. In short, I am afraid all is lost here; and I am grieved to the heart for our dear Queen, who deserves a better fate . . . I hope you will not quit the Mediterranean without taking us . . . I trust in God and you, that we shall destroy those monsters before we go from hence.*[125] Nelson, royalist to the core, was stirred by Emma's letter, 'the picture you draw of the lovely Queen of Naples and the Royal Family would rouse the indignation of the most unfeeling of the creation . . . I am bound – by my oath of chivalry – to protect all who are persecuted and in distress'.[126]

By the end of 1797, the British stood alone against the French. The following May found Nelson on his ship, the *Vanguard*, now damaged in a storm after pursuing the French fleet in the Mediterranean. Now promoted to Rear Admiral of the Blue, Nelson desperately needed information on the French fleet and urgently needed to resupply the ships of his squadron. He had been refused entry to the port of the island of St. Peter so wrote to Hamilton requesting a letter of support from the King issuing orders to the governors of the islands to allow his ships to victual and water at any of the Sicilian ports. His subordinates Troubridge and Hardy went ahead to liaise with the Embassy and obtain the necessary permission.

On hearing the news that Nelson was nearby, anchored off Elba, Emma hastily dashed off a fervent letter; *God Bless you, and send you victorious . . . I will not say how glad I shall be to see you. Indeed I cannot describe to you my feelings on your being so near to us.* The Queen was most anxious to forward notice of her support to Nelson through Emma. *The Queen desires me to say everything that's kind,* Emma assured Nelson *and bids me say with her whole heart and soul she wishes you victory. . . . I send you a letter I have received this moment from the Queen. Kiss it and send it back by Bowen* [Lord St Vincent's messenger to Hamilton], *as I am bound not give any of her letters.*[127]

In 1798, Nelson was placed in command of a special detached squadron of battleships in the Mediterranean. His first task was to intercept the French expedition against Egypt being prepared at Toulon under the command of Bonaparte. However, the British did not know Bonaparte's exact destination, and his 400 transports and 13 battleships sailed on 19 May 1798, evaded Nelson, captured Malta and landed in Egypt on 1 July. However, Nelson discovered the French fleet at Aboukir Bay and destroyed it on 1 August 1798.

Nelson wrote back 'I have kissed the Queen's letter. Pray say I hope for the honor of kissing her hand when no fears will intervene, assure her Majesty that no person has her felicity more than myself at heart and that the sufferings of her family will be a Tower of Strength on the days of Battle, fear not the event, God is with us, God Bless you and Sir William.'[128]

Emma was to add to her list of future claims for recognition that it was due to her influence that the Queen, without the King's knowledge, had provided a letter instructing all governors of the islands to give Nelson the assistance he needed. But in fact it was Hamilton who persuaded Acton to write the order to the governors in the name of the King. With permission granted, Nelson was able to restock his ships at Syracuse and, with his crews rested, was once again ready to give battle. He wrote to Hamilton 'Pray, present my best respects to Lady Hamilton. Tell her I hope to be presented to her crowned with laurel and cypress.'[129]

Nelson finally found the French fleet anchored in Aboukir Bay in Egypt on 1 August 1798, and attacked at once. Some ships of his squadron were able to pass along the unmanned, landward side of the anchored French ships, catching them between two fires. The massive French flagship *L'Orient* exploded and sank, and only two other battleships escaped. The crushing victory at the Battle of the Nile dealt a critical blow to French ambitions in the Mediterranean and the Middle East. Both Nelson and Hamilton recognised that without Emma's help, Nelson might not have obtained his supplies and been unable to go on and defeat the French fleet. Nelson was to write seven years later, on the morning of Trafalgar, 'The British fleet under my command could never have returned the second time to Egypt had not Lady Hamilton's influence with the Queen of Naples caused letters to be wrote to the Governor of Syracuse, that he was to encourage the fleet being supplied with everyting, should they put into port in Sicily. We put into Syracuse and received every supply; went to Egypt and destroyed the French fleet.'[130]

On hearing of Nelson's victory, the whole of Naples erupted in jubilation, the mob 'mad with joy'.[131] The Royal Family were delighted that Nelson had, at least for now, protected them and secured the city. In gratitude, the Queen sent Nelson a letter of congratulation accompanied by casks of wine and a guinea for every man on board. Ecstatic at Nelson's victory, Emma sat down to write him a long gushing letter; *I am delirious with joy, and assure you I have a fevour caused by agitation and pleasure. Good God, what a victory! Never, never has there been anything half so glorious, so compleat.* She fainted when she heard the news and fell on her side hurting herself but declaring dramatically, *but well of that. I shou'd feil it a glory to die in such a cause. No, I wou'd not like to die till I see and embrace the Victor of the Nile.*[132]

In celebration of the great victory, Emma dressed up in a blue shawl covered in golden anchors, with a bandeau around her head embroidered with the words 'Nelson and Victory', with earrings in the shape of Nelson's anchors. Hamilton was no less reverent to his dear friend; 'You have now completely made yourself, my dear Nelson, immortal . . . God be praised . . . You may well conceive . . . how happy Emma and I are in the reflection that is you, Nelson, our bosom friend, that has done such wondrous good.'[133] Despite his victory, Nelson was only raised to the rank of baron rather than viscount or earl, something which angered both Emma and Sir William. Emma wrote to Nelson's wife expressing her anger, *Sir William is in a rage . . . Hang them, I say!*[134] Nelson himself was also bitterly disappointed at the lack of appropriate honours awarded to him.

Badly damaged, on 22 September the *Vanguard* staggered back to Naples carrying Nelson exhausted and wounded. Five years on from their first brief meeting, Nelson was a less able-bodied man; he had lost the sight in one eye at the siege of Calvi in Corsica in July 1794 and he had lost his right arm at Tenerife in July 1797. Concerned about Emma's reaction to his maimed body, Nelson had already written to Emma in August warning her of what to expect; 'I may now be able to shew your ladyship the remains of Horatio Nelson, and I trust my mutilations will not cause me to be less welcome.'[135] The Battle of the Nile had left him with a further wound over his right eye, after a piece of shrapnel had struck him on the forehead. The injury was to leave him with severe headaches for years afterwards.

When Nelson arrived, a great ovation awaited him. The King, Hamilton, Emma and various nobles sailed out to greet him in the Royal Yacht which had been covered in bunting and banners for the occasion. Music regaled them over the water, the bands playing *Rule Britannia* and *See the Conquering Hero Comes* and the crown stood cheering on the bay. Once in earshot, King Ferdinand asked to see the famous hat which had saved Nelson's life, leaving him only with a head wound. The 40-year-old poet Cornelia Knight and her widowed mother were staying with the Hamiltons at the time. Cornelia's mother had been forced to live abroad after the death of husband and her failure to obtain a widow's pension, taking her daughter first to Paris, Toulouse and then to Rome where they lived for eight years. They had recently moved to Naples and were afforded much comfort and protection by Emma and Sir William. Cornelia recalled in her journal, 'Never shall I forget the shouts, the bursts of applause, the toasts, the glasses broken one after another'.[136] The Palazzo was covered in three thousand lamps, and all of Naples were crying '*Nostro Liberatore*', Our Liberator. The Queen was ill and sent her apologies through Emma.

Nelson was greatly touched by the scene, describing it to his wife; 'Alongside came my honoured friends, the scene in the boat was terribly affecting. Up flew her Ladyship and exclaiming *Oh God! Is it possible?* she fell into my arms more dead than alive. Tears however soon set matters to rights; when alongside came the King'. Perhaps rather tactlessly, Nelson relayed the effect Emma had on him to his wife: 'She is one of the very best women in this world. How few could have made the turn she has. She is an honour to her sex and a proof that even reputation may be regained, but I own it requires a great soul.'[137] Nelson had even brought back a Nubian servant girl for Emma, named Fatima.

While on board, Nelson had suffered a serious fever, a recurrence of his earlier malaria; 'For eighteen hours my life was thought to be past hope' he wrote to Lord St. Vincent on 20 September.[138] But better times awaited him as Sir William promised, 'A pleasant apartment is ready for you in my house and Emma is looking out for the softest pillows to repose the few wearied limbs you have left.'[139] At the insistence of the Hamiltons he moved into the Palazzo Sessa where Emma nursed him back to health. She wrote a gloating letter to Nelson's wife; *Lord Nelson is adored here & looked on as the deliverer of this Country he was not well when first he arrived but by nursing & asses milk he went from Naples quite recovered. The*

King & Queen adore him as if he was their Brother, they cou'd not have shown him more respect and attention. I need not tell your Ladyship how happy Sir William & myself are of having an opertunity our dear respectable brave friend return have with [sic] so much honner to himself & glory to his country we only wanted you to be completely happy. Lord Nelsons wound is quite well. According to Emma, she had not only won over Nelson but also Fanny's son, *Josiah is muched improved in every respect we are all delighted with him he is an excellent officer & very steady & one of the Best hearts in the world I love him much & alltho we quarrel sometimes he loves me & does as I wou'd have him.*[140]

Despite his bout of ill-health, before Nelson left Emma insisted on throwing a party in celebration of his fortieth birthday, with 80 diners and 1,740 people at the ball. His stepson Josiah, who had initially taken to Emma, became increasingly resentful as he watched his stepfather's glaringly obvious attentions to her: on one occasion, Josiah became so drunk and abusive that he had to be escorted out of the room. Captain Troubridge, Nelson's friend, looked on in distaste at his public displays of affection for Emma. It was obvious to everyone that Emma was having an effect on Nelson, even to himself. He wrote a confused letter to Lord St Vincent while sat opposite her, apologising, 'Were your Lordship in my place, I much doubt if you could write so well; our hearts and hands must be all in a flutter.'[141] In return, Emma adored Nelson

Thomas Troubridge (1758–1807), had served with Nelson in his early career in the West Indies, and was one of his closest professional friends. In 1798 he was commanding HMS *Culloden* in Nelson's squadron in the Mediterranean. Unfortunately his ship had run aground at Aboukir Bay and he had little part in the Battle of the Nile. He then served as Nelson's deputy during the Neapolitan campaign that followed. However, their friendship was strained when Troubridge warned Nelson of the rumours that were circulating about his relationship with Emma. He was lost when his ship *Blenheim* sank in a storm in 1807.

and was only too eager to bask in his reflected glory. There was little she would not do for him or his fellow seamen; she looked after Captain Hoste who was a guest with them, and she requested a promotion for the messenger Bowen who had carried letters between them. Emma was 34, Nelson was already 40. She had been faithful to Hamilton for 12 years, but it was inevitable she would be attracted to Nelson – both of them aspired to adventure and glory. Hamilton, now 68, was a man she admired and had even grown to love but she had not chosen him. Now for the first time, she had met a man on her own terms with whom she would choose to spend the rest of her life.

Nelson had spent only 23 days with the Hamiltons before he was due to set sail for Malta in mid October. After his departure, both Hamiltons were bereft. Sir William claimed Nelson as 'the friend of our hearts'. Emma gushed to Nelson, *My full heart is fit to burst with pleasure when I hear your honoured name'*. She confessed, *I told her Majesty we onely wanted Lady Nelson to be the female <u>Tria juncta in uno</u>,* ['three in one'] *for we all love you, and yet all three differently, and yet all equally, if you can make that out.*[142] The phrase, *Tria juncta in uno,* taken from the motto of the Order of the Bath to which both Nelson and Hamilton belonged, was to become a shared joke when referring to their own relationship. The relationship between the trio had now melded into a close bond of love and friendship.

Escape from Naples

On 23 November 1798, the King of Naples marched north with 32,000 men in a doomed attempt to protect Rome from the French. Despite this move, the King was still feigning friendship with the invaders, a façade that infuriated the straightforward Nelson. The French, having initially marched straight through the city, reoccupied Rome and took 10,000 Neapolitan prisoners on 5 December, ending all doubt of their intentions to subjugate all of Italy. Those Neapolitans who could, fled, but the French continued marching south intent on taking Naples. The King hastily returned home but with the failure of his expedition the city was now wide open to attack from the French. Dropping all pretence, a second coalition was formed in December 1798 which was to last until 1801 involving Naples, Britain, Russia, Austria, Portugal and Turkey.

By now, Emma and Sir William knew they must leave Naples and urged the Royal Family to start making plans for their escape. In an attempt to persuade the Queen, Emma read her reports from English newspapers describing the seriousness of the situation. Finally, in an impassioned speech, Emma told her what might befall them if they did not leave soon. She wrote to Nelson, *I flatter myself I did much whilst the passions of the Queen were up and agitated, I got up, put out my left arm, like you, spoke the language of truth to her, painting the drooping situation of this fine country, her friends sacrificed & her husband, children, and herself led to the Block, and eternal dishonour to her memory, after for not having been active, doing her duty in fighting bravely to the last to save her country, her*

Religion from the hands of the rapacious murderers of her sister [Marie Antoinette] *and the Royal Family of France, that she was sure of being lost if they were inactive and their was a chance of being saved if they made use of the day, and struck now while all minds are imprest with the Horrers their neighbours are suffering from these Robbers.*[143] For a while, Troubridge stayed with them to offer some protection. Emma was keen to play her role and began organising the evacuation; she declared dramatically that if the Queen was to die at her post, she would remain with her to the last. Promising unswerving loyalty, she scribbled a note on the envelope of her letter to Queen Maria Carolina, *Emma will prove to Maria Carolina that an humble-born Englishwoman can serve a Queen with zeal and true love even at the risk of her life.*[144] Although Emma's declaration might appear theatrical, she did feel obliged to the Queen. She also recognised that she was embarking on an adventure which, if all turned out as planned, would make her a true heroine.

The threat came from two sides; the Neapolitan nobility and middle-class who were thinking about switching sides to the French in the hope they would be allowed to retain their privileges and rights; and the poor, who were tempted by the Liberty, Equality and Fraternity that France purportedly offered. After holding a council meeting, the royal party agreed it was time to remove what valuables they could and make for Sicily. They could see that they had to flee before they suffered the same fate as Louis XVI and Marie Antoinette. However, their departure had to be planned in absolute secrecy in order to avoid inflaming the mob. Any hint that the Royal Family were planning to flee would have resulted in rioting and looting.

In the run-up to the evacuation, Emma acted as go-between for Nelson and the Queen, passing messages between them. Since Emma and the Queen corresponded regularly, letters passing between them aroused no suspicion and for that reason were preferred to official dispatches which might be intercepted. The plan was for the royal household to escape through the tunnels that ran under the embassy and the palace to the shore, taking what valuables they could with them. Linen, silver and jewellery were passed to Emma whose job was to ensure everything was sent onboard the waiting ships. Sir William was also making plans for their departure. He chose his favourite objects from his collection, notably his vases and best pictures, and put them aboard HMS *Colossus* with the intention of selling them to the British Museum. Unfortunately, the ship later sank, taking with it Sir William's treasures, although some were later salvaged. Emma and Sir William were to leave behind three houses with all their furniture as well as all their horses with six or seven carriages.

They were to make their escape one evening during a reception given in Nelson's honour by the Sultan of Turkey, at which Nelson was to be presented with a Plume of Triumph for defeating the French. The plan was for everyone to board the *Vanguard* and set sail for Palermo, but the Royal Family prevaricated, claiming that, for example, some of the treasure-chests had rotted, the children of the household needed to be in bed, and that one of them needed his wet-nurse. Meanwhile, another of the party's ships, the *Alcmene*, was anchored off Posilippo carrying £2.5 million of royal money, waiting to leave as the crowds became increasingly restless, baying for blood and rioting in the streets. Notes flew between Hamilton and Acton, while Nelson became increasingly impatient. He commanded that everyone must be on board by seven o'clock that evening.

The Hamilton party included Sir William, Nelson, Emma, her mother and her servant Fatima; the royal party included the King and Queen, the Princess Royal, two princes, three princesses, and the wife and six-week-old baby of their eldest son. Various servants and nurses were with them, along with a handful of

A portrait of Nelson by Abbott. In his hat he wears The Plume of Triumph, it was presented to him by the Sultan of Turkey for saving Egypt from the French

ministers. They remained anchored for a further two days as a terrible storm blew up. Nelson said it was the worse night that he had seen in 30 years, but feeling unable to wait any longer, put out to sea. Everyone was violently seasick except for Emma and her mother, Mrs Cadogan. Sir William lay in his cabin clutching two loaded pistols and telling Emma that if the ship were to sink he had no intention of awaiting death by drowning. The sickest was the six-year-old prince Carlo Alberto who become gradually worse. Despite Emma's constant nursing, he convulsed and died in her arms on Christmas Day. They finally landed at Palermo on 26 December at 2.00 in the morning. Emma described her adventure to Greville: *not a soul to help me, as the few women her Majesty bought on board were incapable of helping her or the poor royal children. The King and Prince were below in the ward room with Castelcicala, Belmonte, Gravina, Acton and Sir William, my mother there assisting them, all their attendants being so frighte'd and on their knees praying . . . I have been for 12 nights without once closing my eyes . . . thank god we have got our brave Lord Nelson.*[145]

On their arrival in Palermo, the King and Queen moved into the Colli Palace, while Hamilton set up a temporary embassy at the Villa Bastioni. After the initial celebrations, life settled down and the Hamiltons moved to a larger house, the Palazzo Palagonia, near the Mole. The city was now heaving with people, flooded by over 2,000 refugees from Naples. Nelson complained 'Palermo is detestable and we are all unwell and full of sorrow . . . where is it to all end?'[146] As a result of the sudden influx of people, prices rocketed, presenting further problems for those had managed to escape with little or nothing. All of the party were worn out and ill from the horrendous journey. The Queen was inconsolable with grief. Emma lamented, *My adorable Queen whom I love better than any person in the world is allso unwell, we weep together & now that is our onely comfort.*[147] The Queen was obliged to hold a ball of introduction for the nobility of Palermo while overseeing the funeral of her young son. Emma's role in the escape had been reported favourably back in England and she was praised for her courage. Hamilton confirmed to Greville the central role Emma had played, 'Emma has had a very principal part in this delicate business as she is, and has been for several years the real and only confidential friend of the Queen of Naples'.[148] Greville sent his felicitations to Hamilton, 'Tell Lady Hamilton, with my kindest remembrances, that all her friends love her more than ever, and those who did not know her, admire her.'[149] The future of all those involved was still uncertain. Sir William and Emma knew they could not desert the King and Queen while they were still in such distress but planned to leave in the Spring, asking Lord St Vincent to send them a ship to carry them to Gibraltar. Hamilton was in debt having left behind, or lost in the wreck, most of his worldly goods and had to borrow £2,000 from Nelson. Emma was staying up late into the night, drinking and playing cards, her gambling exacerbating their financial problems.

Emma played a significant part in the escape, which had required diplomatic skill, yet her role at this time has been consistently played down. The reasons for this were that she was a woman and one of dubious reputation at that. Emma's marriage to Hamilton had done much to restore her reputation, but now her reversion to her old 'giddy' ways was putting that in danger. She was publicly flirting with Nelson, drinking too much, and gambling recklessly. The collapse of her previous structured life in Naples meant that what discipline Sir William and court life had imposed on her was lost in the chaos of Palermo. Furthermore, against her better judgement, she was falling in love with Nelson and, although she had no wish to purposely hurt Sir William, her guilt at this contributed to her drinking.

Nelson would sit night after night, drinking champagne with Emma and watching her gamble, something he had always previously despised. A concerned Troubridge wrote to Nelson: 'I know you have no pleasure sitting up all night at cards; why then sacrifice your health, comfort, purse, ease, everything to the custom of a country where your stay cannot be long. . . . Lady Hamilton's character will suffer; nothing can prevent people talking. A gambling woman, in the eyes of an Englishman, is lost'.[150] Uninterested, Sir William took to his bed, sick and exhausted from the sea journey. Gossip spread about the trio as it became obvious to everyone that Nelson was besotted with Emma. Lord Keith, Nelson's superior officer, wrote to his sister that Nelson was 'cutting the most absurd figure possible for folly and vanity'.[151]

George Elphinstone, Lord Keith (1745–1823), was a distinguished admiral who in 1798 was appointed second-in-command of the Mediterranean Fleet under Lord St Vincent. When St Vincent returned to England in June 1799, Lord Keith replaced him and for the first time Nelson came under his command. His fixation on affairs (of all kinds!) at Naples lead Nelson to neglect the wider Mediterranean picture, causing friction with his commander-in-chief who was not sad to see him go in 1800. Lord Keith commanded in the North Sea and the Channel later in the Napoleonic Wars, and it was to one of his ships, the *Bellerophon*, that Napoleon surrendered in 1815.

While they were in Palermo, the French took over Naples on 23 January 1799, setting up the Parthenopean Republic assisted by the middle-class anti-monarchists and former royal officials. The *lazzaroni* continued to fight against the French, while the wealthy Neapolitans were siding with them. Violence and looting was rife throughout the town and atrocities were commonplace with little evidence of any control. Some of the 2,500 French troops were garrisoned at the Hamiltons' houses, damaging the beautiful treasures they had had to abandon.

In May, Nelson heard that the French fleet had left Brest, so made plans to combine his ships with those of Lord St Vincent, Troubridge and Duckworth to engage them. After he had left,

Emma and Sir William confessed that they missed him more than ever; 'I can assure you' wrote Sir William, 'that neither Emma nor I knew how much we loved you until this separation, and we are convinced your Lordship feels the same as we do.'[152] Nelson wrote in response, 'To tell you how dreary and uncomfortable from the *Vanguard* appears, is only telling you what it is to go from the pleasantest society to a solitary cell, or from the dearest friends to no friends . . . You and good Sir William have spoiled me for any place but you.'[153] So close had the three grown at this stage that Nelson drew up a codicil to his will in May 1799, the first of many. To Emma, he left a small box encrusted with diamonds, a gift he had received from the Sultan's mother; and to Sir William 50 guineas for a memorial ring.[154] The amiable relationship between Nelson and Hamilton was based on mutual admiration and respect; Hamilton said of Nelson, 'He is the most humane and active man I ever met with.'[155] Hamilton's deep feelings for Nelson and his love for Emma led him to tolerate the affair taking place under his own roof – he wanted to lose neither of them, referring to them both as his best friends. Emma still cared deeply for Hamilton and would do anything to spare him pain. Regardless of her love for Nelson, she did not want to desert the kindly old husband who had treated her with so much compassion throughout her life. The strength of this bond between the two men allowed them to share their passion for Emma. Thus began a most intriguing *ménage à trois* which was to last for seven years.

On 13 June 1799, news arrived in Palermo that Cardinal Fabrizio Ruffo's army had liberated Naples from the French. But in order to avoid further bloodshed, Ruffo had exceeded his authority and granted an armistice to the rebels. Disgusted with such leniency, the King and Queen immediately requested that Nelson return to Naples and end Ruffo's agreement. At this point, Lord Keith ordered Nelson to go and defend Minorca, a command which he chose to ignore. Nelson was determined to stay and defend the Kingdom of Naples, at the risk of Minorca if necessary, believing that it was his sacred duty to protect the Royal Family and the Hamiltons, and so he set sail aboard the *Foudroyant* to restore order in Naples, taking with him Emma and Sir William as translator and adviser. The three shared living accommodation, thrown together in cramped living quarters, with little privacy between them. There was no possibility of returning to the Palazzo Sessa as it had been ransacked. *I saw at a distance our despoil'd house in town & Villa Emma that had been plunder'd & Sir Wm's new apartment, a bomb burst in it,* she told Greville *but it made me so low-spirited I don't desire to go again.*[156] All three of them were in a state of nervous tension; Nelson had been suffering from headaches on and off and felt wretched through lack of sleep; Sir William had been ill with various bilious fevers and his rheumatism was bothering him; and Emma's attention was focused on Nelson, and although tense, she was in a state of high excitement.

Nelson's ships arrived at Naples on 24 June to find the city in chaos. It had been looted by rioters, sacked by the invading French, and then been pillaged yet again by the so-called liberators. Under Ruffo's agreement, there was no distinction made between the French and the Neapolitan rebels; the French were to be allowed to departed with honours, and the Neapolitans to remain in Naples without retaliation against them. Ruffo was essentially a humanitarian and had negotiated to prevent further bloodshed but the terms of the agreement were to be overruled. Instead, the King and Queen called for brutal reprisals; in a letter to Emma, the Queen demanded severe punishment: 'The rebel patriots must lay down their arms and surrender at discretion to the pleasure of the King. Then, in my opinion, an example should be made of some of the leaders of the representatives, and the others to be transported under pain of death if they return into the dominions of the King . . .'[157]

Nelson issued a warning to the rebels to 'submit to the King's clemency' under 'pain of death'.[158] When they refused, he decided to take whatever measures were necessary to re-establish royal authority. A fort was taken with the loss of some 500 men. The rebel chosen for execution as a public example was Commodore

The Royal palace at Castello Covo on the Bay of Naples

Francesco Caracciolo. He had long served in the Neapolitan navy, fleeing with the Royal Family on the same ship to Palermo but had returned to Naples, taking sides with the republicans. Despite his entreaties that he be shot rather than hanged like a common criminal, Nelson was implacable, and Caracciolo was hanged from the yardarm of his own ship the *Minerva*, his body being left to swing there before a cheering crowd for two hours before it was thrown into the sea. Despite this being the only execution he was responsible for, Nelson was accused of inhumanity. Lady Holland condemned both Nelson and Emma's actions, reporting scathingly: 'Lord Nelson had brought back the fugitive monarch to his capital, and Naples now exhibits a scene of revenge, more bloody than the Sicilian Vespers. The hearts of Frenchmen are brought as trophies to a cruel people, who crouched in servile subjection whilst they were too abject to fight in their own cause. Lady Hamilton has not been remiss in adding her quota to the barbarity which enflames every breast.'[159] What Emma actually thought of these proceedings is unknown, but she was bombarded with petitions from alleged traitors pleading with her to intercede for mercy on their behalf. Writing to Emma's mother in Palermo, Nelson complained, 'Our dear Lady . . . has her time so much taken up with excuses from rebels, Jacobins, and fools, that she is every day most heartily tired.'[160] Emma met with the head of the loyal *lazzaroni* who offered 90,000 supporters but complained that only 20 of them bore arms. Nelson supplied them with sufficient weapons and another 100 marines in order to protect the city until the King arrived. Fourteen days after the trio's arrival, the King joined them in Naples but would not come ashore, preferring to stay on the *Foudroyant*, while the Queen remained in Palermo. Emma was in her element, caught up in a situation where others were looking to her for help. She boasted to Greville; *The Queen is not yet come. She sent me as her Deputy; for I am very popular, speak the Neapolitan language, and [am] considered, with Sir William, a friend of the people.*[161] Sir William continued to praise Emma's political acumen to Greville, 'Emma makes a great figure in our political line, for she carries on the business with the Queen, whose abilities you know are great.'[162] Having given up their cabins to the King, Emma and Sir William were now confined to one room below deck. At midday every day, they dined with the King and, while he slept, they sat down to write. According to her mother's wishes, after her death on 20 July, Cornelia Knight had placed herself under the protection of the Hamiltons. She kept Emma company and helped her to organise her correspondence but constant translating for the King and Nelson had left Emma exhausted, Nelson complaining that she was 'fretting [her] guts to fiddle-strings'[163] as a result of her concern for Maria Carolina.

After regaining control of the situation in Naples, the party landed back in Palermo in triumph on 8 August. The streets were thronged with crowds welcoming them with cries of *Viva Nelson! Viva Miledi! Viva Hamilton!* Emma had a dress specially made for the celebrations of the feast of St Rosalia, the patron Saint of Palermo; the material was embossed with motifs of 'Nelson-Bronte-Nelson', the Dukedom of Bronte having been awarded to Nelson by a grateful King Ferdinand. Nelson was now a hero all over again and dressed the part in full regalia, adorned with his Turkish Plume of Triumph and all his medals. Songs were sung about them, fireworks lit up the sky, 21-gun salutes were fired from the castles, and illuminations hung on a vessel kitted out as a Roman galley with a rostrum dedicated to Emma showing her picture supported by two angels. Fancy dress balls and masquerades were held, Emma dressed to one ball as 'Favourite from the Hareem,' to mock their detractors who were already gossiping about her affair with Nelson. In appreciation of their loyalty, the Queen showered the trio with presents. Emma and Sir William were given jewellery worst approximately £6,000 for their help during the ordeal; Emma received a fine gold chain with the Queen's miniature; Hamilton received a huge yellow diamond ring;

Lady Hamilton.
Peinte à l'âge de 30 Ans,
par le célèbre Romney.

An engraving of Emma at 30

and Nelson was given a diamond-encrusted sword owned by Louis XIV. The British government at last rewarded him for his endeavours – £2,000 and a gift of £10,000 from the East India Company for securing their trade routes by his defeat of the French fleet. Emma was now confidently in charge and organising her life as she saw fit. Visiting Palermo, Lady Elgin remarked on how Nelson was 'now completely managed by Lady Hamilton'. She also commented on Emma's broadening figure, 'She looked very handsome at dinner, quite in an undress; – my father would say, "There is a fine woman for you, good flesh and blood." She is indeed a Whapper! and I think her manner very vulgar'.[164] However, Emma kindly offered her an apartment there. For Nelson, their triumph had been at a cost. Lord Elgin noticed how old Nelson looked and that he had lost all his upper teeth.[165]

As he sailed to Leghorn to meet with Lord Keith, now incensed enough to demand Nelson join him, Nelson wrote his first love letter to Emma; 'no Separation, no time, my only beloved Emma can alter my love and affection for You' he declared, 'it is founded on the truest principles of honour, and it only remains for us to regret which I do with bitterest anguish that there are any obstacles to our being united in the closet ties of this World's rigid rules, as We are in those of real love. Continue only to love Your faithful Nelson as he loves his Emma'. Nelson and Emma had evidently become sexually intimate by now. Although he had only been away a couple of weeks, he was already love-sick. 'I can neither Eat or Sleep for thinking of You my dearest love, I never touch even pudding. You

Thomas, Earl of Elgin (1766–1841), is best remembered for acquiring the marble sculptures adorning the frieze of the Parthenon in Athens, when he was ambassador at the court of the Turkish sultan, who ruled Greece at the time. Over a decade he brought them home, only to sell them to the government in 1816 for £35,000. They are now the most famous exhibit in the British Museum.

know the reason. No I would starve sooner. My only hope is to find You have Equally kept Your Promises to Me . . . but I rest perfectly confident in the reality of Your love and that You would sooner die than be false in the smallest thing to Your Own faithful Nelson who lives only for his Emma . . . I shall run Mad.' He dreamt of her '. . . You came in and, taking Me to Your embrace whispered "I love nothing but You My Nelson". I kissed You fervently And we enjoyed the height of love. Ah Emma I pour my Soul to You . . . no love is like Mine toward You.'[166] Referring to this time, Nelson was later to recall, 'Ah my dear friend, I did remember well the 12th February, and also the two months afterwards. I shall never forget them, and never be sorry for the consequences.'[167] Lord Keith again issued orders to Nelson to sail and assist in the blockade of Malta but Nelson, claiming ill health, rushed back to Palermo to be with Emma. On 24 March 1800, the *Foudroyant* returned to the blockade of Malta without him. Seemingly unaware of the harm being done to both their reputations, Emma wrote to Greville, *We are more united and comfortable than ever, in spite of the infamous Jacobin newspapers jealous of Lord Nelson's glory and Sir William's and mine. But we do not mind them Lord N. is a truly vertous man; and because we have been fagging, and ruining our health, and sacrificing every comfort in the cause of loyalty, our private characters are to be stabbed in the dark . . . So I beg you will contradict any of these vile reports.* According to Emma, *Sir W. and lord N. live like brothers.*[168] Hamilton wrote, 'Ld Nelson + I with Emma are the *Tria Juncta in uno*'.[169] At Nelson's request, Emma was awarded the Maltese Cross by Tsar Paul of Russia for her services in assisting the starving Maltese, the only time it had ever been given to an English woman. Emma wrote to Greville, *I have rendered some service to the poor Maltese. I got them ten thousand pounds and sent them corn when they were in distress.*[170] As a reward, the Queen had the cross set in diamonds for her.

In April 1800, after 36 years of service to his country, Hamilton was recalled. His time as ambassador to Naples was over. By May, Nelson had also received his summons home and they began to make sad preparations for the journey. All of them were to be sorely missed by the many friends they had made there over the years. Lord Bristol lamented the leaving of Emma; 'I am so indebted to you', he wrote to her, 'and you deserve so much to be loved, that my gratitude and sincere friendship will last till my tomb. God bless you in your long travels.'[171] Annoyed at being continually disobeyed by Nelson, Lord Keith refused to give them leave to sail home in a British ship, retorting that Lady Hamilton had had command of the fleet for long enough. Undeterred, the party made a farewell tour in the *Foudroyant* from Palermo to Malta, calling in at Syracuse. While aboard, they celebrated Emma's birthday by throwing a party in Nelson's cabin. Cornelia Knight composed a song for the celebration, where Emma sang and played the harp.

The trio finally set off for England in the summer, travelling via Austria accompanying the Royal Party; this included not only Maria Carolina, but three princesses, two princes and 50 of her retainers. By this time Emma was pregnant. Although her plumpness disguised her pregnancy for a while, Sir William must have noticed his wife's condition. Her body was changing and she was growing larger by the month. Emma certainly did not want to give up her marriage after struggling so hard to win 'respectability'. Nelson seems to have been happy about the fact that she was going to give him his first child. Although his wife had a son by her first husband, she never had children by Nelson. The three of them continued as if nothing had happened.

Emma preferred to make the long trip by land, seemingly impervious to the plight of those around her. Cornelia Knight wrote to Captain Berry, 'It is at length decided that we go by land and I feel all the dangers and difficulties to which we shall be exposed . . . Lord Nelson is going on an expedition he disapproves . . . Lady Hamilton . . . hates the sea, and wished to visit the different Courts in Germany, Sir William says he will die by the way, and he looks so ill that I should no be surprised if he did.'[172] They sailed as far as Leghorn where they attended a state reception ceremony for the Queen in the cathedral and proceeded on land to Florence for a couple of days. Increasingly concerned about the presence of French troops, after passing within two miles of them at one point, they also had to endure the dreadful condition of the roads. At Castle San Giovanni, the coach carrying Emma, Sir William and Nelson overturned giving them all a fright but none of them were severely injured. With their own carriage broken, they took over that of Cornelia and Mrs Cadogan while the coach was repaired. Having met up again, from Ancona they all made their way by sea on Russian frigates – the royal family, Emma, Nelson and Sir William in one, followed by Cornelia and Mrs Cadogan in another. The voyage was blighted once more as Hamilton fell ill, along with the Queen and 43 of her party.

In Vienna, they were feted; the court threw banquets on their behalf, concerts were arranged for them, and firework displays filled the skies. They frequently dined with up to 60 people at a time and amused themselves with operas, hunting and visiting, remaining for six weeks. They called on Lord and Lady Minto, the latter remarking about Nelson, 'He is devoted to Emma, thinks her quite an angel, and talks of her as such to her face and behind her back, and she leads him about like a keeper with a bear. She must sit by him at dinner to cut his meat, and he carries her pocket-handkerchief'.[173] Sir William had a relapse. A concerned Lord Minto commented, 'I cannot see how it is possible for him to reach England alive'.[174] Along with many others, Lord Minto was critical of Nelson's behaviour; 'he does not seem at all conscious of the sort of discredit he has fallen into, or the cause of it, for he writes still not wisely about Lady Hamilton and all that. But it is hard to condemn and use ill a hero, as he is in his element, for being foolish about a woman who has art enough to make fools of many wiser than an Admiral.'[175] Emma was also the target of derision; after a ball at Prince Esterhazy's, Lord FitzHarris was rude enough to remark of her, 'Lady Hamilton is, without exception, the most coarse, ill-mannered, disagreeable women we meet with.'[176]

The Queen was bereft at the impending separation from Emma, and Emma herself admitted, *I am miserable to leave my dearest friend. She cannot be consoled.*[177] As a parting gift, Maria Carolina gave her a diamond necklace enlaced with the royal children's initials made from the tresses of their hair; to Sir William she gave a golden snuff box, the lid inlaid with portraits of the King and Queen. Taking leave of the Queen in Vienna, they went to Prague and then on to Dresden where Emma was snubbed by the Electress of Saxony who refused to receive her. This perhaps should have warned Emma as to the reception she might receive on her return to English society.

The trio were coming in for repeated attacks. Mrs Melesina St George who was visiting Lord Minto's brother Hugh Elliot and his wife in Dresden at the same time as Emma's party remarked, 'It is plain that Lord Nelson thinks of nothing but Lady Hamilton, who is totally occupied by the same object. She is bold, forward, coarse, assuming and vain. Her figure is colossal, but excepting her feet, which are hideous, well shaped.'[178] She also nicknamed Emma and Nelson, 'Anthony and Moll Cleopatra', and noted that Emma was guzzling champagne in great quantities. Hugh Elliot and his wife were disgusted with Emma's raucous behaviour and her penchant for her mother's Irish stew; they mocked poor 70-year-old Sir William's dancing and sneered at Nelson's excitable nature, even accusing him of being drunk. Years later, Nelson's nephew was to deny this, recalling his uncle as a sober, quiet gentleman. Arriving in Hamburg, Emma met the poet Friedrich Gottlieb Kloptock and, with a display of typical bravado, showed off her Attitudes despite being six months pregnant. For the last leg of the journey, they caught a packet boat, the *King George*, and landed at Yarmouth on 6 November.

Back in England

Nelson received a hero's welcome in England. Bells rang out for his landing at Yarmouth, pubs changed their names in acknowledgement of their hero and medals were struck to commemorate his return. A thanksgiving service was held and Nelson was given the freedom of the city. From the docks, Nelson, Emma and Hamilton took a carriage to Nelson's house in Roundwood, Ipswich but on their arrival, there was no-one there to greet them. They were expecting Fanny and Nelson's father to be there but found they had already left for London planning to meet Nelson there. While Cornelia Knight and Mrs Cadogan went off to stay in a hotel in Albemarle Street, Nelson, Emma and Sir William made their way to Nerot's hotel in King Street where they found Fanny and Nelson's father waiting for them (Cornelia Knight, who had travelled back with them, refers to a hotel in Albemarle Street in her autobiography, while Greville mentions that he left his name for them at Nerot's hotel in King Street).[179]

That evening as the Hamiltons and the Nelsons sat down to dine together at Nerot's, the two women eyed each other up but were pleasant enough to one another. Fanny, although not sure quite what was going on, was quick to pick up on how attentive Nelson was to Emma. She must have had her suspicions as satirical cartoons of Nelson and Emma were already circulating in London. Despite this, everyone ignored the reality of the situation and continued to act as though everything was normal. Greville shuddered at this state of affairs and shared his concerns about his uncle's reputation with Joseph Banks – he 'hoped to put him out

Gillray's caricature of Emma and Nelson smoking is full of sexual innuendo. Their pipe is purposely given a phallic shape

of the line of ridicule' but felt he would be unable to 'help him to the comfort and credit to which his character and good qualities entitle him'.[180] Yet Lord Palmerston noted that Emma and Sir William were as close as ever, always talking about Nelson 'and Sir William says his friendship and connection with him is the pride and glory of his life'.[181] Evidently his best friend's relationship with his wife had not diminished the regard Hamilton held for him.

In the long term, Nelson had already forwarded instructions to his prize agent and close friend Alexander Davison that lodgings be organised for himself and his wife in London while William Beckford had offered the Hamiltons his house in Grosvenor Square. The Hamiltons and the Nelsons made a point of being seen together in public; they attended the theatre together applauded by the audience who sang *Rule Britannia*. The *Morning Herald* reported their night out on 19 November 1800; 'Lady Hamilton is rather *embonpoint* but her person is nevertheless graceful and her face extremely pretty. She wore a blue satin gown and head dress worth a fine plume of feathers'. Emma had taken to wearing her dresses highly-waisted at this time, as was the fashion, rather convenient for hiding her pregnancy. Lord Palmerston noted the changes, 'She has grown much larger and her face broader and her features stronger than they were. She was dressed in a white wrapping gown which made her look of very large dimensions, but so completely took away all her shape that I cannot judge what her figure would be in a common dress.'[182] While visiting the theatre, Emma met up with her friend the actress Jane Powell again. Fits of fainting took place, with the two women vying for attention. The *Morning Herald* reported 'about the end of the third act Lady Nelson fainted away and was obliged to be carried out of her box'. During another evening out, Emma fainted. Nelson immediately rushed to her side, giving his wife a clue as to the situation. Fanny was further enlightened as to Emma's condition when, dining together one night, Emma suddenly left the table. Fanny remained in her seat waiting for Emma to compose herself and return but was severely reprimanded by Nelson for not showing enough concern for her guest. To the surprise of their other guests, Nelson stalked out after Emma to offer her his assistance. Embarrassed, Fanny left the table to seek out Emma only to find her being sick in a basin. With every incident, Nelson's displays of irritation were increasing; at a dinner given in his honour at Admiralty House, when Fanny tried to assist him by shelling some walnuts for him, he rejected her offer with such violence that he smashed a glass. One evening, a cataclysmic row broke out at the Nelson house. In despair, Nelson rushed out into the street, undecided whether to go to the Hamiltons or not. In the end he knocked on their door, hurried into their house and threw himself down on their couch, complaining '. . . I have no real friends out of your house'.[183] The Hamiltons took him in and from then on, the three were to live together until Sir William's death; to his credit Hamilton admitted he did not give ' . . . a fig for the world. I have lived too long to mind what the world either thinks or says on such matters'[184] – he understood that gossip surrounded them but he recognised that their happiness lay in ensuring the three of them stayed together.

The trio were in for a series of rebuffs. On their return, Nelson and Sir William were invited to go to court and be received by King George III. Given all their services to their country in Naples, they could have at least expected some praise or recognition from the King, but instead he made a point of snubbing them both. After a quick introduction, he turned his back and gave his attention to another less important guest. Although the King may have been scandalised at the gossip surrounding the men, and had never liked or accepted Emma, it was poor thanks for all the years of diplomatic work Hamilton had put in, and no consolation for the injuries Nelson had endured. Meanwhile Emma, who had yearned to be accepted at the English court, was still refused audience with the Queen. The gossip intensified and people were beginning to refuse invitations to dine at the Hamiltons as a result. Advised by Troubridge, Cornelia Knight distanced herself from them for fear of being rejected by polite society. Emma, having looked after Cornelia for two years since her mother's death, was understandably upset, calling her *dirty ill-bred ungrateful, badnamed false and deceitful.* Nelson was less subtle, thereafter referring to her as 'That Bitch Miss Knight'.[185]

The trio went off to spend Christmas with William Beckford at Fonthill, a distraught Fanny being left behind to take care of Nelson's father. The eccentric Beckford had built a Gothic abbey in the grounds of his home, Splendens, at Fonthill and was now in a position to show it off. On Christmas Eve a procession of carriages, horses, soldiers and guests were moved from the old house to the abbey; 'Flambeaux, torches, and many thousand lamps were distributed on the sides of the road among the woods;

whilst bands of music and files of soldiers were stationed in different places to greet and charm the company as they passed. Everything indeed was provided to steal upon the senses, to dazzle the eye, and to bewilder the fancy. After passing through a long, winding, umbrageous avenue, after hearing the sounds of distant, near, and varied instruments, with their reverberations among the woods and dells . . . the company was conducted to the abbey where a new impressive, and mystical scene, or succession of scenes, were presented.' A monastic-style meal awaited them in the Cardinal's Parlour served up in enormous silver platters. After dinner they all went to the apartments in the abbey, the staircase lit with large wax torches. Emma once again displayed her Attitudes and sang along with Madame Banti whom she knew from Naples. Flattering Emma, Beckford declared, 'You must shine steadily . . . that light alone which beams from your image, ever before my fancy, like a vision of the Madonna della Gloria . . .'.[186]

Nelson was recalled to Plymouth on 17 January 1801, after his appointment as Vice Admiral of the Blue, second-in-command of

Gillray satirised Emma's increasing weight and anguish at Nelson's departure with the fleet in his cartoon *Dido in Despair*

the Channel Fleet under Sir Hyde Parker. This occasioned yet another satirical cartoon, Gillray's *Dido in Despair*, depicting a very fat Emma tearing her hair in despair at Nelson's leave-taking. Sir William, now suffering public ridicule, was satirised as a cuckold. His earlier fear of such mockery had been expressed to Greville on the outset of his affair, 'It would be fine fun for the young English travellers to endeavour to cuckold the old Gentleman their Ambassador, and whether they succeeded or not would surely give me uneasiness.'[187] This was now unfortunately coming to pass. Another satirical depiction, Gillray's *A Cognocenti contemplating ye Beauties of ye Antique,* caricatured Nelson as Mark Anthony with the unfaithful Emma as Cleopatra clutching a bottle of gin, her drinking now common knowledge.

On 29 January 1801, Emma gave birth at home to a healthy baby girl. The birth itself must

The cartoons of James Gillray (1756–1815) were so savagely satirical and such up-to-the-minutes critiques of the political and social scene of his time, that people used to gather outside the shop of his publisher, Mrs Humphrey, in St James's Street to buy the latest prints as they came off the press. His most famous subjects were George IV, whose self-indulgence Gillray exposed mercilessly, and the prime minister, William Pitt, whose rectitude he ridiculed.

have been fairly unproblematic as three days later, she was already up and about. Conscious of the gossip, she attended a grand concert held at the Duke of Norfolk's house as though nothing had happened. It seems impossible that Hamilton did not know that she had given birth under his own roof. Evidently, he preferred to ignore it and tactfully appeared oblivious while Emma took to her bed with a feigned illness. Three weeks after the birth, he wrote to Nelson about Emma 'all her convulsive complaints certainly proceed from a foul stomach' and 'she is much better – having vomited naturally, and is now purposing to take a regular of tartar emetic.'[188] This was Sir William's tactful way of letting Nelson know that Emma had recovered from the birth and was out of danger. Emma called the baby Horatia after Nelson and placed her into the care of a nurse, Mrs Gibson, at 9 Little Titchfield Street. Mary, Mrs Gibson's daughter, recalled the event over 27 years later, revealing to Horatia's brother-in-law, Captain Philip Ward, that 'Lady Hamilton brought the child to her mother's house in a hackney coach one night, and placed her under her charge telling her that she should be handsomely remunerated. She was unattended and did not give the nurse any information as to the child's parents. The nurse declared she was no more than eight days old. She remained with the nurse until she was five or six years old. The event took place either in January or February 1801; and Mrs Gibson said she could never make out why Horatia's birthday was kept on 29 October'.[189] The reason was, in fact, to give the impression that the child had been given into their protection while abroad, thus distancing them as the real parents. Horatia remained with the nurse until she was five or six years old but Emma frequently visited, often accompanied by Nelson who played for hours with the infant on the floor.

Nelson was frantic with worry prior to the birth and wrote to Emma at least once a day. To protect their identity, they wrote of their domestic situation and feelings for each other under the guise of a concocted a story about a fictitious crew member called Thomson (or Thompson – the spelling varied) who had left to go to sea leaving his pregnant lover in Emma's care. Both of them were worried that their love letters would fall into the wrong hands. Nelson was to burn all of Emma's letters in order to protect her reputation, such as it was, and ordered Emma to do the same but she could not bring herself to dispose of them. Nelson was ecstatic when he heard that 'Thompson's child' had been born safely. Using her code name, he wrote to her, 'I believe dear Mrs Thomson's friend will go mad with joy. He cries, prays and performs all tricks yet dares not show all or any of his feeling, but he has only me to consult with.'[190] He promised to drain a bumper of wine to the health of 'Mrs Thomson' but ended up drinking two along with Troubridge, Hardy, Parker and his brother. He swears she is 'his only, only love', that he will marry her as soon as possible, ' . . . and that you must [at] every opportunity kiss and bless for him his dear little girl, which he wishes to be called Emma, out of gratitude to our dear, good Lady Hamilton, but in either case . . . he leaves to your judgement and choice.' He declared he would marry her instantly if her 'uncle' Hamilton were to die. All of Nelson's letters are filled with adoration of Emma and concern for their child; 'I sit down . . . to write you a line: not to assure you of his eternal love and affection for you and his dear child, but only to say that he is well and as happy as he can be separated from all he holds dear in this world. He has no thoughts separated from you love and your interest. They are united . . . one fate, one destiny . . . '[191] To prove his commitment, Nelson made a will on 4 February 1801, leaving Emma the £2,000 owed to him by Sir William. He also left Emma his portrait of Maria Carolina which she had given him on their parting, and set up a trust fund for Horatia. In order to conceal her parentage, Emma and Nelson were to bring up Horatia as 'godparents', the child supposedly entrusted to their care. Nelson wrote to Emma about the christening of their child; 'Its name will be Horatia, daughter of Johem and Morata Etnorb. If you read the surname backwards, and take the letters of the other names, it will make, very extraordinary, the names of your real and affectionate friends, Lady Hamilton and myself'.[192]

Nelson was insanely jealous of the recent attentions shown to Emma by the Prince of Wales who was vying for an invitation to visit the Hamiltons. The Prince by now had a notorious reputation as a result of the countless affairs he had conducted with various infamous women. He now pressed Sir William for an invitation to dinner. On hearing this, Nelson became incensed, crazed with worry that the Prince would seduce Emma. A flurry of letters to Emma ensued in February expressing his concerns; 'I know his [the Prince of Wales] aim is to have you for a mistress . . . I am in tears, I cannot bear it.' He told her the prince was 'without one spark of honour' but ' . . . know you too well not to be convinced you cannot be seduced by any prince in Europe'. Despite saying he trusted her, he nonetheless had his doubts; 'I own I sometimes fear that you will not be so true to me as I am to you, yet I cannot, will not believe, you can be false . . . I hope to be dead before that should happen'. Despite his declaration that he could 'write nothing', he sent her angst-ridden diatribes dramatically announcing, 'I am more dead than alive'. Nelson, well aware of the Prince's rakish behaviour, was keen for Emma to defend her honour. To this end, he issued strict instructions regarding the impending visit from the flirtatious Prince, 'Do not sit too long at table. Good God! He will be next to you, and telling you soft things. If he does, tell it out at table, and turn him out of the house. Oh God! that I was dead! . . . I am almost mad but you cannot help it.'[193] Nelson had worked himself up into a state of nervous distress. At one point, having convinced himself that Emma would fall for the Prince, he declared melodramatically ' . . . don't forget that you once had a Nelson, a friend, dear friend, but alas! . . . he has lost the best, his only friend, his only love. Don't forget him, poor fellow!'[194] In the end, Emma stood 'firm as a rock', taking to her bed with a fictitious ailment in order to avoid the potentially risky situation.

Hamilton too was no stranger to the slippery ways of the flirtatious Prince, but he recognised that it would not do to fall out of favour with him, particularly while he was pressing the government for a pension and compensation for his losses in Naples. He wrote to Nelson telling him how, although they had contrived to avoid such a commitment, the prince had insisted he wanted to hear Emma sing with Banti. 'In short, we will get rid of it as well as we can, and guard against its producing more meeting of the same sort. <u>Emma would really have gone to any lengths to have avoided Sunday's dinner.</u> But <u>I thought it not prudent</u> to break with the Prince of Wales.' Kindly, Sir William goes out of his way to pacify Nelson's and allay his anxieties. 'I have been thus explicit because I know well your Lordship's way of thinking, and your kind attachment to us and to everything that concerns us.'[195]

George IV (1762–1830) ruled as prince regent from 1811 and as king from 1820. He was the most dissolute of all British monarchs and is best remembered for his building projects, above all the Royal Pavilion at Brighton. In 1785 he married Mrs Fitzherbert, a Catholic widow. If the marriage had not been illegal it would have ruled him out of succeeding to the throne. Ten years later he gave into pressure and married his cousin, Caroline of Brunswick. The couple separated soon after the birth of their daughter and he tried unsuccessfully to divorce her. She was barred from his coronation, an embarrassing situation resolved by her death three weeks later.

The sexual side to Nelson and Emma's relationship was constantly expressed through Nelson's letters. He delighted in lascivious banter and described all his lusty thoughts to her. In one note, remembering a previous evening with her, he exclaimed 'Would to God I had dined alone with you. <u>What a desert [*sic*] we would have had</u>'.[196] His amorous thoughts excitedly tumbled out, 'What must be my sensation at the idea of sleeping with you! It setts me on fire . . . I am sure my love & desires are all to you, and if any woman naked were to come to me, even as I am this moment thinking of you, I hope it might rott off if I would touch her even with my hand.'[197] He assured her he would be faithful and the thought of their having more children together pleased him; writing in the third person he added optimistically, 'I daresay twins will again be the fruit of your and his meeting. The thought is too much to bear. Have the dear thatched cottage [her pubic hair and vagina] ready to receive him and I answer that he would not give it up for a Queen and a palace'.[198] (This mention of twins has raised some conjecture that Horatia may have been one of twins, but there is no other evidence for this.)

Nelson had been brought up to be a religious man but had managed to reconcile his faith and the desertion of his wife by seeing Emma and himself as being married before God. He called her, 'my own dear wife', adding 'for such you are in my eyes and in the face of heaven'. He frequently contemplated the possibility of a future for them both as a happily married couple, but for this he had to consider the death of Hamilton; 'You know, my dearest Emma, that there is nothing in this world that I would not do for us to live together, and to have our dear child with us . . . we must manage till we can quit this country or your uncle dies. I love, I never did love anyone else.' He promised, 'I worship, nay, adore you, and if you was single, and I found you under a hedge, I would instantly marry you.'[199] Significantly, it appears that Emma never told him about the child she had borne in her youth; 'I never had a dear pledge of love till you gave me one, and you than God, never gave one to anyone else.'[200] Emma was too emotionally involved to dare risk telling Nelson the truth; even though Hamilton was paying for the child's upkeep, it is unlikely even he was told the real identity of the child's mother, although he probably guessed.

Finally Nelson's ships arrived at Portsmouth for repairs on 23 February 1801, and Nelson hurried back to Emma. He had only three fleeting but passionate days with her. Nelson's sister-in-law had been staying with her but had just left before he arrived. Emma wrote sympathetically, *How unlucky you went so soon.*[201] Knowing he was due to leave, Emma lamented, *My heart is fit to burst quite with grief. Oh, what pain, God only knows . . . I shall go mad with grief.*[202] Despite his short leave, Nelson raced to see his daughter at Titchfield Street. On leaving for Yarmouth, Nelson invited Sir William and Emma to come and see him off. Sir William, now under the influence of his not so affable nephew Greville, declined. He was tired, he had had enough of travelling and was grateful for time with Emma alone.

Nelson had become resentful of his wife and wanted her out of his life so he could concentrate solely on his devotion to Emma. He had responded bitterly when Emma mentioned Fanny in a letter to him, 'Let her go to Briton [Brighton] or where she pleases, I care not; she is a great fool, and thank God! you are not the least bit like her.'[203] Yet his allowance of £1,800 a year to her was extremely generous. He maybe felt some guilt as she had always been a loyal and faithful wife to him. Meanwhile, Emma had done her best to ingratiate herself with Nelson's family who tended to side with her against Fanny. His sisters were all now her closest confidantes. Sarah, Nelson's sister-in-law, frequently shared gossip about Nelson's wife referring to her as 'Tom Tit' because of her bird-like gait. *Tomtit does not come to town.* Emma reported,

Nelson kept this miniature of Emma with him at all times

She offered to go down but was refused. She only wanted to go to do mischief to all the great Jove [Nelson]'s *relations. 'Tis now shown all her ill treatment and bad heart. Jove found it out.*[204]

Fanny continued to try and wheedle herself back into her husband's affections, pleading, 'Let me beg, nay entreat you, to believe no Wife ever felt greater affection for a Husband than I do, and to the best of my knowledge I have invariably done everything you desire. If I have omitted anything, I am sorry for it'.[205] Despite the fact that she has been depicted as a cold and unfeeling woman, she still loved Nelson, was evidently a devoted wife and uncomplainingly took on the task of looking after his ailing father. She proposed a meeting with Nelson in London but he immediately rebuffed her with a terse note effectively telling her he was separating from her for good, 'Living, I have done all in my power for you. And if dead you will find I have done the same. Therefore, my only wish is to be left to myself, and wishing you every happiness, believe that I am your affectionate Nelson and Bronte.'[206]

Financial problems were looming for both Nelson and Sir William. Nelson concentrated on trying to reclaim some of the prize money obtained by Lord St Vincent for the victories they had won. Sir William faced his own difficulties having lost most of what he owned in the rush to escape from Naples. Emma had had to sell off her diamonds to enable them to buy furniture for their rented house at 23 Piccadilly only a few months after their return. Their strained financial circumstances were further eased by Sir William's decision to sell off his collection at Christies in March 1801, which brought in £5,000[207] although the pension of £4,000 he was awarded from the government was only half of what he thought he would receive in compensation for his losses at Naples. Madam Le Brun's portrait of Emma as a bacchante was among the items sold and Nelson was infuriated since this was one of his favourite

Emma as a bacchante before Vesuvius. Painted by Elisabeth Louise Vigee le Brun in 1792. This portrait was Nelson's favourite image of her by any artist

portraits of Emma; 'I see clearly, my dearest friend, you are on SALE', he wrote to Emma on 11 March 1801.[208] He did, however, manage to purchase Romney's portrait of her as St Cecelia which was also up for sale for £300, and hung the painting in his cabin. Nelson gave instructions for all his future mail to be forwarded to Emma and added a codicil to his will on 6 March 1801, adding £1,000 per annum. In yet another codicil, he bequeathed her his diamond star and three diamond boxes.[209]

Nelson prepared for battle. Denmark was hindering the British blockade of France and the British fleet were under orders to persuade Denmark, either by force or agreement to withdraw from an alliance formed with Prussia, Sweden and Russia, as part of an 'Armed Neutrality of the North'. Emma hurriedly wrote a note to Nelson before the battle; *Our dear glorious friend, immortal and great Nelson, what shall I say to you this day? My heart and feelings are so overpowered that I cannot give vent to my full soul to tell you, as an Englishwoman gratefull to her country's saviour, what I feel towards you.*[210] Emma never reproached him for leaving her but urged him on, knowing she would bask in his reflected glory. Before going into battle, he wrote to her, 'He has no fear of death but parting from you.'[211]

The battle at Copenhagen on 2 April 1801 gave rise to one of the legends surrounding Nelson. During the attack on the Danish fleet, he was serving under Sir Hyde Parker's command. Parker had witnessed the difficulties his fleet was in and had given the signal to withdraw. Nelson, determined nothing should come between him and winning the battle, decided to ignore the orders. Placing the telescope to his sightless eye, he declared, 'I really do not see the signal'.[212] Fortunately, he went on to win the battle and became a viscount in recognition of his services in spite of Parker's call for his court martial. Missing Nelson, Emma composed a poem for him:

Silent grief, and sad forebodings
(Lest I ne'er should see him more),
Fill my heart when gallant Nelson
Hoists Blue Peter at the fore.[213]

After his success, Nelson landed at Yarmouth on 1 July and quickly made his way back to the Hamiltons, exhausted after his campaigns. After he had rested, Emma took Nelson and Hamilton off for a trip to the country, staying at the Bush Inn in Staines and the Fox and Hounds at Burford Bridge accompanied by William Nelson and his wife Sarah, their daughter Charlotte, and Nelson's favourite young protégé, Edward Parker. Their holiday was to be brief as news of a potential French invasion arrived and Nelson was quickly recalled to duty. In command of the *Medusa* with orders to protect the British coast, by the beginning of August he was sailing toward Boulogne to attack the French shipping. He made two attacks on the enemy but these achieved little. A couple of months later, much to Nelson's distress, his 21-year-old protégé Parker was wounded off Boulogne. On his return, Sir William and Emma went down to Deal to visit Nelson, staying at the Three Kings Inn. While there, Emma helped Nelson tend the boy as he lay dying in hospital. Nelson insisted on paying all the expenses for his lodgings and the surgeon as the boy's father could not afford it. Emma left with Hamilton for London, leaving Nelson forlorn, 'I came on board but no Emma. No, no my heart will break I am in silent distraction . . . My dearest wife, how can I bear our separation? Good God, what a change.'[214] Nelson was now tired and drained. He had long been mulling over the idea of buying a haven so the three of them could spend the rest of there days together. He sent word to Emma to look for a place for them.

Merton and the Death of Nelson

No longer living with Fanny, Nelson now needed a permanent residence of his own, a place to which Emma and he could retreat. Before returning to sea after another brief leave, he instructed Emma to look for a suitable home for them. After careful searching, she found a quaint cottage in Merton, Surrey, for a total of £9,000 and bought it on Nelson's behalf, £3,000 being forwarded by Davison as a down payment.[215] The grounds held a canal, a small tributary of the River Wandle, which they were to nickname 'the Nile' after Nelson's victory, and in which Sir William could indulge his passion for fishing. They had finally found a place they could all call home.

Despite her delight in finding their new idyll, Emma was upset because Sir William had refused to allow her relatives to stay with them while they were visiting London. After receiving her complaints, Nelson told her, 'I trust the farm will make you more so [happy] than a dull London life. Make what use you please of it. It is as much yours as if you bought it. Therefore if your relatives cannot stay in your house in town, surely Sir William can have no objection to your taking to the farm: the pride of the Hamiltons surely cannot be hurt by settling down with any of your relations; you have as much right for your relations to come into the house as his could have.'[216] Emma was to take up his offer and from then on, the place would be filled on and off with both her own and Nelson's extended family.

Looking forward to their new life in the country, Emma and Sir William took up residence in the newly purchased cottage in

October 1801 to await Nelson's return. The survey on the house had not been promising – it was dilapidated and too small, with too little land. Nonetheless, Emma was overjoyed with it and set about its refurbishment; new water closets were fitted, and the rooms were furnished and embellished with mirrors and glass. Much to the amusement of Sir William, Emma and her mother set about building pigsties and hen-coops, even supplying ducks for the river. All this was a drain on Nelson's resources yet he complimented Emma on her thriftiness, declaring, 'You will make us rich in your economies'.[217] This was somewhat incongruous given Emma's extravagance and shows the extent of Nelson's infatuation with her, seeming impervious to her faults. Nonetheless, Merton was a good investment and Nelson seized the opportunity to buy the surrounding land. Sir William insisted that the expenses were shared during time spent together at Merton; he was also spending beyond his means, but was not yet prepared to give up his London house.

A sketch of Merton House by Thomas Baxter

Nelson had put in for sick leave after suffering constant toothache, seasickness and bowel trouble, as well as being feverish. After four months at sea, he at last returned to Merton to rest and recover. He was exhausted as Emma reported to his sister *I am sorry to tell you I do not think our dear Lord Nelson well, he . . . is sickening & low & throws himself on the sofa <u>tired and says I am worn out</u>.*[218] Yet they were all contented. Emma nursed the fatigued Nelson back to health and he took his seat in the House of Lords.

All three of them made frequent trips to London; Emma went on shopping expeditions with Mrs William Nelson, Nelson attended to naval business at the Admiralty, and Sir William went to the auction rooms and to the British Museum regarding his antiquities. Merton was increasingly full of friends and relatives with all of the Nelson family frequent visitors and Emma took both of William Nelson's children under her wing.

Fourteen-year-old Charlotte came down on a regular half-day holiday and sat with Sir William while he caught the occasional pike in the river. Emma gave her French and Italian lessons as well as entertained her with outings and gifts. Both Charlotte and her brother Horace stayed at Merton when on holiday from school, and Nelson paid for Horace's schooling at Eton and for his clothes. They all regularly attended services at the local parish church together and gradually settled into the community. Occasionally, Emma instructed Mr Gibson to bring Horatia on

Horatia as an infant

one of her many visits to Merton but generally she was still kept at a distance for the sake of discretion. Old naval friends began dropping in, including Fady, the boy who Emma had nursed in 1798, now a charming young man. Emma concerned herself with assisting Nelson's servants and ship crew wherever she could, and Nelson relied on her to look after his family and their dependants; after his brother Maurice died, leaving a bereft widow, Nelson told Emma; 'I am sure you will comfort poor blind Mrs Nelson'.[219] She also offered to take in Maurice's old black servant, James Price.

Although Emma enjoyed lavish entertainment, she knew Nelson despised high society socialising and was happier entertaining in his own home. With this in mind, she did her best to create a convivial atmosphere, inviting Nelson's father down to Merton in November. This was his first visit and although he was polite to Emma, his loyalties lay with Nelson's ex-wife. Other family members descended for Christmas; Mrs Matcham and her eight children, the Boltons with their six children, and the William Nelsons and their two children. Musicians, thespians and nobility were invited down – old friends Mrs Lind, Mrs Denis and Mr Billington dropped in, as well as Hayley. Even royalty visited – Prince Leopold, Maria Carolina' son and Prince Castelcicala, the Neapolitan Ambassador's son came to see them. Emma quickly made friends of her new neighbours and their families; the rich Jewish art patron Abraham Goldsmid, Captain Cook's cousin Isaac Smith, the journalist James Perry, and the Halfhides and the Newtons, families who lived close by. Despite being shunned by 'polite' society and the Court, Emma was enjoying herself throwing smaller parties but continued to spend extravagantly. Their expenses were increasing by the week and both Nelson and Hamilton were concerned but were not prepared to put a stop to her spending.

Lord Minto arrived in February, a friend of Nelson who had long since taken a dislike to Emma. He immediately hated Merton and complained that Emma had filled it to the brim with

Nelson memorabilia – cups, plates and tributes to Nelson, as well as both their portraits all over the house. Minto thought it tasteless to express such admiration for a man in his own home and accused the Hamiltons of living off Nelson, which was far from the truth. 'The whole establishment and way of life is such as to make me angry as well as melancholy', he complained, 'nothing shall ever enduce me to give the smallest countenance to Lady Hamilton. She looks ultimately to the chance of marriage . . . in the meanwhile, Sir William, and the whole set of them are living with him at his expense. She is in high looks but more immense than ever. She goes on cramming Nelson with trowel-fuls of flattery which he goes on taking as quietly as a child does pap. The love she make to him is not only ridiculous but disgusting.'[220] Such was his hypocrisy that Emma was unaware of his dislike for her and considered him a good friend. Matters finally came to a head as a result of Emma's spending and her continuous round of entertaining. It had all become too much for Hamilton and it was clear that he had had enough of life at Merton. He complained to Greville, 'It is but reasonable, after having fagged all my life, that my last days should pass off comfortably & quietly. Nothing at present disturbs me but my debt, and the nonsense I am obliged to submit to here to avoid coming to an explosion, which wou'd be attended with many disagreeable effects, and wou'd totally destroy the comfort of the best man and the best friend I have in the world. However, I am determined that my quiet shall not be disturbed, let the nonsensical world go on as it will.'[221]

Emma's birthday was overshadowed with the news of the illness of Nelson's father a couple of days earlier. Yet the day had its joys seeing the christening of Emma's 20-year-old Nubian servant Fatima at the parish church, where she took the name Fatima Emma Charlotte Nelson Hamilton. Nelson's father died the following day and Hamilton was quick to sympathise; 'Emma says I must write to you of condolence for the heavy loss your lordship has suffered . . . in the case of your good father, the lamp was suffered to burn out fairly, and that his suffering were not great; and that by his son's glorious and unparalleled success, he saw his family ennobled . . . '.[222] Nelson felt unable to attend the funeral for fear of upsetting Fanny who had nursed the old man through his last illness. Meanwhile, Nelson's own health had worsened and he had to consult a surgeon about his eyes. Reminded of his own mortality by his father's death, he made another will in May 1801, leaving the Merton cottage to Emma. Knowing Emma's generosity and her tendency for extravagance, he had justified concerns that she would fall into poverty after his death. Another death, that of Romney, Emma's loyal friend who had painted her image so many times, added to their grief.

Needing a break, the trio set out on a three-month tour of Wales in July 1802, ostensibly to visit Hamilton's estates at Milford Haven but also as a triumphal tour for Nelson. The William Nelsons accompanied them, first calling in at Oxford to meet up with the Matchams. Nelson received the freedom of the city, and both Hamilton and Nelson received Honorary Degrees in Civil Law, while William Nelson received a Doctorate of Divinity (he already had one from Cambridge). They went on to visit the Duke of Marlborough at Blenheim Palace but suffered a disappointing blow as he refused to receive them. Much to Emma's disgust, they were merely offered a cold luncheon in the grounds which they sharply refused and promptly left. Elsewhere throughout their travels they gained enthusiastic reception in every town they visited – Monmouth, Milford, Swansea, Cardiff – where cheering crowds greeted them and applauded. Emma revelled in the attention and was delighted when invitations poured in from every quarter. Emma wrote triumphantly to Davison, *We have had a most charming Tour which will Burst some of them* [with envy].[223] She was revelling in all the attention.

Now in his seventies, Hamilton was old and tired. Constant bickering with Emma was wearing him down. Rather than confront each other face to face, despite the fact that they were living under the same roof, they dealt with their problems in letters. By August, Sir William had had enough of touring and wanted to go back home but Emma became irritable as she wanted to go to Ramsgate to bathe. Also she had privately instructed Mrs Gibson to bring Horatia to nearby Margate so she could discreetly visit her but had lost the address of their lodgings. She became increasingly agitated at the thought of missing them and her annoyance was taken out unfairly on Sir William. She facetiously remarked, *As I see it is pain to you to remain here, let me beg of you to fix your time for going. Weather I dye in Piccadilly or any other spot in England, 'tis the same to me; but I remember the time when you wished for tranquillity, but now all visiting and bustle is to your liking.*[224] He responded patiently, but pointedly, 'I neither love bustle nor great company, but I like some employment and diversion but I have a very short time to live, and every moment is precious to me. I am in no hurry, and am exceedingly glad to give every satisfaction to our best friend, our dear Lord Nelson. Sea-bathing is useful to your health; I see it is, and wish you to continue a little longer; but I must confess I regret whilst the season is favourable, that I cannot enjoy my favourite amusement of quiet fishing. I care not a pin for the great world, and am attached to no-one as much as you'. She replied *I go, when you tell me the coach is ready.* He responded hurt, 'This is not a fair answer to a fair confession of mine'.[225]

Sir William did his best to explain his feelings at some length to Emma in order to try and reach a compromise. He had grown weary of the constant round of entertaining; 'I am arrived at the age when some repose is really necessary, & I promised myself a quiet home, and although I was sensible, & said so when I married, that I would be superannuated when my wife wou'd be in her full beauty and vigour of youth; that time has arrived, and we must make the best of it for the comfort of both parties . . . I by no means wish to live in solitary retreat, but to have seldom less than 12 or 14 at table & those varying continually, is coming back to what was become so irksome to me in Italy during the latter years of my residence in that country'. He felt hurt and neglected, bereft of her attentions which were now given over entirely to Nelson; 'I have no complaint to make, but I feel that the whole attention of my wife is given to Ld N and his interest in Merton. I well know the purity of Ld N's friendship for Emma and me and I know how uncomfortable it would make his Lp, our best friend if a separation shou'd take place . . .'.[226] He was determined to avoid such a thing and hoped that the mere mention of it would be enough to quieten Emma down. It worked for a while, and they continued in a more harmonious household.

When Sir William died on 6 April 1803, both Nelson and Emma were at his bedside. In Hamilton, Emma had found the father-figure that she had never had, as well as a life-long companion and devoted husband. Her grief for Hamilton was real and anguished. She left a note that same day, *Unhappy day for the forlorn Emma. Ten minutes past ten dear blessed Sir William left me.*[227] Nelson wrote, 'Our dear Sir William died at 10 minutes past Ten this morning in Lady Hamilton's and my arms without a sigh or struggle. Poor Lady H. as you may expect is desolate. I hope she will be left properly, but I doubt it.'[228] Nelson was correct about her inheritance: Hamilton had indeed left the bulk of his estate to Greville. Although Hamilton had provided adequately enough for Emma to live comfortably if she reigned herself in, he knew as well as Nelson that this was most unlikely. The settlement was ungenerous considering the assets he left behind; he left Emma a lump sum of £3,000 and an annuity of £800 which included a yearly provision of £100 for her mother. He had also agreed to pay off Emma's debts of £700, having advanced £250 for this, the rest to be paid of by the arrears of his pension owed to him by the government. Somewhat optimistically, Hamilton had asked Greville to request that the King continue to pay his pension to Emma after his own death; she never received it, nor could he have really expected it.

Nelson was not alone in his astonishment at the inadequacy of the provision for Emma. Even Elliot who despised Emma declared, 'Worse off than I imagined'. Maria Carolina also condemned the relative smallness of his bequest, seeing Emma as 'so indifferently provided for'.[229] For 'his dearest friend' Nelson, Hamilton left a copy of Madame le Brun's portrait of Emma in enamel by Bone, 'a very small token of the great regard I have for his Lordship, the most virtuous, loyal and truly brave character I have ever met with. God bless him and shame fall on all those who do not say "Amen"' – Hamilton was finally giving Emma to Nelson. To protect Emma's interest, Nelson advised that the Deed of Gift of furniture to Emma be read in front of the family or it might be assumed that Greville had given her the furniture which she had actually paid for.[230] Hamilton was buried in Pembrokeshire, laid beside his first wife at his request. Neither Nelson nor Emma attended the funeral. Instead Emma fitted out her household in black at a cost of £185, and ornamented it with jet or black enamel for another £170.

Both Nelson and Emma wrote various applications in an attempt to obtain a pension for her. On 13 April, she petitioned the Prime Minister for a portion of Sir William's pension; at the same time she wrote to Lord Addington for a private pension in her own right and compensation. She found herself 'in circumstance far below those in which the goodness' of Sir William had kept her. She declared, . . . *what is well known to the then administration at home – how I too strove to do all I could towards the service of our King and Country. The fleet itself, I can truly say, could not have got into Sicily but for what I was happily able to do with the Queen of Naples (and through her secret instructions so obtained), on which depended the refitting of the*

fleet in Sicily, and with that all which foiled so gloriously at the Nile.[231]
Only a month after Hamilton's death, Greville served notice to quit on Emma at 23 Piccadilly, being part of the estate left to him by his uncle. He then deducted tax from her annuity leaving her with less than Hamilton had intended. Nelson was to write from the *Victory*, 'Greville is a shabby fellow! It never could have been the intention for Sir William but that you shou'd have had seven hundred pound a year in neat money'.[232] In his favour, despite his meanness, Greville did keep his promise to Sir William, and wrote to support her applications for a pension. Even now, Emma was not willing to forego her London base and moved all her furniture to a new house she had found at 11 Clarges Street.

Emma and Nelson had only been together for 18 months before war broke out again and Nelson was recalled to duty. They had time to ensure Horatia was baptised but neither Emma nor Nelson attended. To avoid gossip, they left the arrangements for the christening to Mrs Gibson, including instructions to remove the name from the register. But at her baptism on 13 May 1803, this was not done and the name Horatia Nelson Thomson was left in, with Lady Hamilton and Lord Nelson given as her godparents; her date of birth was incorrectly given as 29 October 1800 to preserve the pretence of her adoption in Italy. A few days later, Emma presided over the wedding of Captain William Bolton to his cousin, Nelson's niece Kitty Bolton with the reception at Emma's house in Clarges Street.

One by one the countries of the Second Coalition had fallen to France and in March 1802 Britain had been forced to sign the Peace of Amiens. As hostilities broke out again in May the following year as a result of Napoleon's quest for Empire in Europe, a third coalition was formed which included Prussia, England, Austria, Russia and Sweden. Nelson had been given command in the Mediterranean aboard his flagship HMS *Victory* and went to blockade Toulon with the intention of preventing the French and

Miniature of Saint Emma

Spanish fleets meeting up, since their combined force could cover an invasion of England. His departure left Emma even more bereft than before, now without the comforting companionship of Sir William. As soon as he left, he dashed off a letter while travelling down to Portsmouth, 'Cheer up, dearest Emma, and be assured that I ever have been and am and ever will be, your most faithful and affectionate.'[233] The hint of impending doom was ever-present in his letters when he went into battle. A few days later he comforted her, 'I feel from my soul that God is good, and in his due wisdom, will unite us.' In his cabin, gazing at the portrait of 'Santa Emma' and little Horatia, Nelson's thoughts were continually of Merton and home.[234]

Despite Nelson's generous allowance of £100 a month for the upkeep of Merton, Emma's spending was out of control, partly a result of her loyalty and generosity to her relatives and old friends, the most extravagant example of which was a £2,000 loan to the Connors which she could not expect them to repay. With his debts escalating, yet unwilling or unable to reign in Emma's spending, Nelson agreed for her to undertake even more renovations at Merton. Seemingly the highest priority for him was the protection of his daughter's welfare, as he instructed Emma to fit a three-foot netting around the 'Nile' so that Horatia might not fall in.

While Nelson was away, their second child 'Emma' was born in February 1804 but only lived for six weeks. Emma wrote to Nelson to let him know how ill they had all been, herself, Horatia and baby Emma, but that the baby had died. Nelson wept but was grateful Emma and Horatia had been saved, 'I was in such agitation! At last I found one [a letter] without a date, which, thank God! Told my poor heart that you was recovering, but that dear little Emma was no more! And that Horatia had been so very ill – it all together upset me . . . I am sure the loss of one – much more both – would have drove me mad . . .'[235] Suffering from depression after losing her child, Emma missed Nelson and pleaded with him to be allowed to let her come out and see him in the Mediterranean. He refused to let her join him knowing she would be safer at home, but endeavoured to keep her entertained with gossip from his visit to Naples; Maria Carolina had been instructed by Napoleon to dismiss Acton; the King no longer loved his wife; and bad news – their old friend, Lord Bristol now separated from his wife, had died in Rome in July the previous year (1803) after a stomach complaint. By this time the 46-year-old Nelson's own health was failing; his sight had worsened, and he was blighted with a chronic cough. Worried about lack of news about Nelson, Emma's skin complaint flared up so she went to Southend to bathe in the sea. As a further distraction from fretting about Nelson, she visited to the Boltons in Norfolk and the William Nelsons in Canterbury where William had, on Nelson's recommendations, at last obtained his Prebendary at the Cathedral.

Nelson wrote to Emma from the *Victory* on 13 August 1804: 'I am now going to state a thing to you, and to request your kind assistance, which, from my dear Emma's goodness of heart, I am sure of her acquiescence in. Before we left Italy, I told you of the extraordinary circumstances of a child being left to my care and protection. On your first coming to England, I presented you the child, dear Horatia. You became, to my comfort, attached to it, so did Sir William, thinking her the finest child he had ever seen. She has become of that age when it is necessary to remove her from a mere nurse, and to think of educating her. Horatia is by no means destitute of a fortune. My earnest wish is that you would take her to Merton, and if Miss Connor will become her tutoress under your eye, I shall be made happy.'[236] The pair had contrived the idea of pretending Horatia was Nelson's godchild placed under Emma's care in order to explain her suddenly taking up residence at Merton. Even so, there was some difficulty in executing Nelson's plans for Horatia to live permanently at Merton. In November 1804, Horatia was still with Mrs Gibson. By May 1805, Nelson had his solicitor write to Mrs Gibson as he thought she was reluctant to give back Horatia. He offered her a yearly allowance of £20 if she handed over the child immediately and had nothing more to do with her. Although Nelson presumed it was due to Mrs Gibson's reluctance to give up Horatia, it might well have been Emma's disinclination to be permanently fettered with a child; even then, Emma often failed to pay her for her daughter's upkeep. She might even have been jealous of Nelson's attention towards Horatia as it is evident that he was more affectionate towards his daughter than Emma was. He had insisted on her being vaccinated against smallpox and refused her a dog because of fear of her catching rabies. Emma might also have foreseen the clashes she would have with her daughter. Horatia had a temper, a predisposition to her mother's temperament, which Nelson recognised, 'Ay, she is like her mother: will have her own way or kick up the devil of a dust'.[237]

As Nelson was about to return, Emma abided by his wishes and brought their daughter back to Merton, taking on Sarah Connor as her governess. Nelson had willed Horatia £4,000 left in trust in order she might gain an acceptable place in society. This he knew must be prevented from falling into Emma's hands but she was allowed to oversee the interest. Emma continued to pour money into improvements at Merton, and her constant round of trips to visit relatives and to the seaside increased her expenses. While she was away, her mother wrote to her 'My Dear

A sketch of Emma seated at Merton by Thomas Baxter

Emma, Cribb is quite distrest for money, would be glad if you could bring him the £13 that he paid for the taxes, to pay the mowers . . . I have got the baker's and butcher' bills cast up; they come to one hundred pound seventeen shillings'.[238] Emma was still gambling and her losses were mounting; one friend paid off debts of £530 but she continued to spend.

Meanwhile, Nelson was chasing the French, missing them and becoming increasingly frustrated. Recalled, he landed on 19 August 1805 having been away for two years and three months. Emma hurriedly wrote to all the family, the Nelsons, the Boltons and the Matchams, inviting them all to Merton for Nelson's home-coming. The Boltons immediately left for Merton, but the Matchams were delayed as Kitty's child William had just died and she was indisposed by grief. Once Nelson was home, Emma insisted on entertaining visitors, including Beckford, Lord Minto, Admiral Sir Sidney Smith and the Duke of Clarence (later William IV). Minto noticed that the passion between Emma and Nelson was 'as hot as ever'.[239]

Nelson went up to town to confer with ministers about the war. Soon after, Captain Henry Blackwood called on him at Merton with the Prime Minister's request that Nelson immediately return to sea. After only 25 days together, Emma was distraught at the thought of his leaving so soon. She knew there was little point in trying to keep him at home, nor would she have wanted to as she shared his lust for glory. In a letter to Scott she was to write, *Did I ever keep him at home? did I not share in his glory? Even this last fatal victory, it was I bid him go forth. Did he not pat me on the back and call me brave Emma, and said, 'If there were more Emmas, there would be more Nelsons'.*[240] Nelson feelings for Emma were equally bound to his duty and doing battle; 'The call of our country is a duty which you deservedly, in the cool moments of reflection, reprobate, was I to abandon:', he told Emma, 'and I should feel so disgraced by seeing you ashamed of me! No longer saying, "This is the man who saved his country!"'. His ambition was to save his country for his 'wife in the eyes of God'.[241] Nelson had long since recognised this fighting quality in Emma and her ability to spur people on in times of adversity, her strength and enthusiasm affecting him greatly; he had told Dr Mosley on the *Victory*, 'Her Ladyship's . . . inexpressible goodness to me is not to be told by words, and it ought to stimulate me to the noblest actions; and I feel it will'.[242]

Emma always understood his talents and pressed him on to greater successes. Nonetheless, it was not easy for her, as she explained to one of the Bolton sisters: *I am again broken-hearted as our dear Nelson is immediately going. It seems as though I have had a fright's dream and am awoke to all the misery of this cruel separation. But what can I do? His powerful arm is of much consequence to his country.*[243] Lord Minto was a guest on 12 September, the night before Nelson was due to leave for Portsmouth; 'Lady Hamilton was in tears all day yesterday' he commented, 'could not eat, hardly drink, and near swooning, and all at table. It is a strange picture. She tells me nothing can be more pure and ardent than this flame.'[244]

Nelson took his leave on 13 September 1805, saying a prayer over Horatia, now nearly five, as she lay asleep. He had doted on her, showering her in expensive gifts – a rocking horse, silver cutlery with her name engraved, and a special drinking-cup 'To my much-loved Horatia' and wondered when he would see her again. Taking stock of his life as he travelled down to meet his fleet, Nelson could see that his health was gone and this was perhaps the last battle he would fight. He wrote in his pocket book 'Friday night, at half past ten, drove from dear, dear Merton, where I left all that I hold dear in this world, to go to serve my King and country. May the great God whom I adore enable me to fulfil the expectations of my country, and if it is His good pleasure that I should return, my thanks will never cease being offered up to the throne of His mercy.'[245] He had left Emma knowing, in all likelihood, he would not return. Emma was prostrate with grief. Mrs Cadogan was holding the fort as usual, busying herself with daily activities. Charlotte Nelson was on hand to give comfort. She helped Horatia write her last letter to her father to which he responded, 'My Dearest Angel, I was made happy by the pleasure of receiving your letter . . . and I rejoice to hear that you are so very good a girl and love my Dear Lady Hamilton who most dearly loves you, give her a kiss from me . . . you are ever uppermost in my thoughts'.[246] Emma went with Charlotte to stay with the William Nelsons in Canterbury, leaving Horatia with Miss O'Connor. Missing her daughter, Emma wrote to Nelson on 4 and 8 October; *My heart is broke away from her, but I have now had her so long at Merton, that my heart cannot bear to be without her . . . Oh! Nelson, how I love her, but how do I idolise you – the dearest husband of my heart, you are all in this world to your Emma. May God send you victory, and home to your Emma, Horatia and paradise Merton, for when you are there it will be paradise.*[247] Emma's mother and Mary Connor, her sister's replacement as governess, wrote to Emma reporting on Horatia's daily life. She was now learning French and Italian.

Horatia portrayed as a bacchante before Vesuvius with perhaps less of the glamour and enthusiasm of her mother Emma in a similar portrait

Emma returned to Merton and after only a few days sent for Susannah Bolton to keep her company.

On board ship, Nelson attended to the last codicil to his will, his 'Bequest to the Nation'. In it, he acknowledged Emma's services to her country; first that she obtained the King of Spain's letters to Ferdinand telling him of his intentions to declare war on England; second, that 'the British fleet, under my command, could never have returned the second time to Egypt, had not Lady Hamilton's influence with the Queen of Naples, caused letters to be wrote to the Governor of Syracuse, that he was to encourage the fleet being supplied with everything,' Finally he commended Emma and Horatia to his King and Country requesting they make provision for them; 'Could I have rewarded those services, I would now call upon my Country, but as that had not been in my power, I leave Lady Emma Hamilton, therefore, a Legacy to my King & Country, that they will give her an ample provision to maintain her rank in life. I also leave to the benefice of my Country my adopted daughter, Horatia Nelson Thompson, and I desire She will use in the future the name of Nelson only. These are the only favours I ask of my King and Country at this moment when I am going to fight their Battle.'[248] Sadly, both would let Nelson down.

Nelson's fleet was off Cadiz, waiting for the combined Franco-Spanish fleet to sail, and at 6.00am on 21 October 1805, the two fleets sighted each other off Cape Trafalgar. Before going into battle, Nelson put on his uniform coat pinned with every medal he had won, and took his position on deck. Captain Hardy, Nelson's friend and flag captain who would remain a close adviser to Emma, urged him to change it as he was making it easy for the enemy sharp-shooters to see who he was, but Nelson refused. At the height of the battle he was hit by a bullet through the shoulder which shattered his spine. As he was carried down to the surgeon by his faithful shipmates, he covered his face so the

Nelson on the deck of the Victory at Trafalgar

crew could not see he was hit. On his desk lay his last letter to Emma; 'My dearest, beloved Emma, the dear friend of my bosom, the signal had been made that the enemies' combined fleet are coming out of port . . . May the God of Battles crown my endeavours with success; at all events I will take care that my name shall ever be most dear to you and Horatia, both of whom I love as much as my own life; and as my last writing before the battle will be to you, so I hope in God that I shall live to finish my letter after the battle, May Heaven bless you prays your Nelson and Bronte . . .'.[249]

Life after Nelson

Bells chimed and cheers rang out on 6 November 1805 as news spread that the Battle of Trafalgar had been won on 21 October, but the celebrations were combined with an outpouring of national grief for the death of Nelson. From the *Victory*, Scott had written to Mrs Cadogan to prepare Emma for the worst. But as the horses pulled up at Merton, it was Captain Whitby who had the task of telling Emma that Nelson was dead. Hearing the reports of the battle, Lady Elizabeth Foster immediately rushed to her friend's side. She recalled Emma's reaction to the news in her diary; Emma had taken to bed, attended to by Mrs Bolton, as she was unwell with a rash, *They brought me word, Mr Whitby, from the Admiralty. Show him in directly I said, he came in, and with a pale*

Nelson's grand funeral processes up the Thames

Nelson's funeral carriage reaches St Paul's

countenance and faint voice said, ' We have gained a great Victory.'
'Never mind your victory', I said, ' My letters – give me my letters – Capt.
Whitby was unable to speak – tears in his eyes and a deathly paleness
over his face made me comprehend him. I believe I gave one scream and fell
back, and for about ten hours after I could not speak nor shed a tear –
days have passed on, and I know now how they should begin or end – nor
how I am to bear my future existence.[250] Nelson's nephew, George
Matcham, still a young boy, never left her side for days, trying to
encourage her to eat and take medicine.

When Nelson's body finally reached England, Kitty, Nelson's
favourite sister, had a death mask made. Had he lived, Nelson had
every intention of retiring to his Beloved Emma and Paradise
Merton. After Nelson's body had lain in state at Greenwich, Scott
accompanied it to St Paul's Cathedral where the funeral took
place. The authorities had tried to prevent the Prince of Wales

attending but he was determined to go. Thousands of people lined the streets as the funeral car passed through London in an unprecedented show of national mourning. Emma was not invited to the funeral and did not attend.

Prostrate with grief, Emma lay in bed for weeks surrounded by Nelson's letters. On 29 November 1805, she wrote *Life to me is not worth having. I lived for him. His glory, I gloried in; it was my pride that he should go forth; and this fatal and last time he went, I persuaded him to it. But I cannot go on. My heart and head are gone.*[251] Condolences from friends did little to ease her grief. In an attempt to cheer her up, Susannah Bolton invited her down to their farm at Cranwich. Hardy came bearing Nelson's hair, his shoe buckles and his last letter to her. At the bottom, she scribbled *Oh Miserable wretched Emma! O Glorious & happy Nelson.*[252]

For the last seven years, her whole life had centred around Nelson and now at 40, a life without him seemed empty. If her loss was not bad enough, the bulk of Nelson's inheritance went to his brother William. Yet it was typical of Emma to think about other people and, even while indisposed with grief, she asked her mother to write to the government requesting they look after Nelson's family. In gratitude for Nelson's services, the government showered gifts and awards on his relatives while Emma and Horatia were ignored. Nelson's brother was made an earl and his nephew Horace made a viscount – yet in life, Nelson had only been made a viscount. The title brought his brother £5,000 a year and a gift of £120,000. Even his sisters received £10,000 each (later increased to £15,000) and his estranged wife a pension of £2,000 per year. All in all his family received £200,000. William Nelson, so quick to drop Fanny in favour of Emma, now thought it prudent to abandon Emma in turn, although his wife Sarah, now a Countess, would visit her despite the difficulties Emma had with William's meanness. The Boltons and the Matchams remained loyal and stayed on good terms with her; she went to stay with the Boltons repeatedly and the young girls, Eliza and Anne, idolised her. Her friends Ladies Elizabeth Foster, Percival and Abercorn, also came to offer their condolences and comfort Emma. Yet although the Nelson's sisters liked Emma and stuck by her, none of them seem to have thought it proper to provide Emma and their niece with an income from their newly-found wealth.

Nelson had done his best to protect Emma. She owned the house at Merton and all the furniture inside as well as that at Clarges Street. She was supposed to receive £800 per annum from Hamilton' estate, a £2,000 gift from Nelson and a £500 annuity but most of this failed to materialise.[253] Mrs Cadogan wrote to her urging her to obtain a solicitor to ensure Earl Nelson was sorting out Nelson's will, but a month later, her bills remained unpaid; her mother wrote to her again more urgently, 'My dear Emma, I owe Marian 4 months wages which is 2 guineas. I had it not to give her, & she wants shoes & stockings. If you can give Sarah Connor thirty shillings to pay her washerwoman as she is indebted to her for three months washing.' She apologised that she had no money with which to buy Emma a birthday present.[254]

Nearly a year after Nelson's death, in November 1806, William Nelson had still not acted upon Nelson's last codicil to his will and Emma had to write to him urging to pay her. He even went to Merton to see what papers he could find and only with the utmost reluctance handed over the coat Nelson had worn at Trafalgar to Emma. He instructed his wife to write to Emma: 'The coat which our beloved lamented Lord had on when he received his fatal wound is as you know in our possession – in point of right there can be no doubt as to whom this precious relick belongs, & it certainly is my Lord's most ardent wish as well as my son's who spoke very feelingly on the subject before he left us . . . My Lord is willing & tho' done with a bleeding heart, to part with it to you',[255] on the proviso she return it to his heir for preservation later. William Nelson failed to make any payment, initially stating that income from the Bronte estate up to 1806 was for arrears of rent, and he did not in fact pay her anything until 1808. Even then the money was not paid in advance as advised in the will, until 1814. Emma summed up his miserliness some years later writing to Scott from near Calais, *Think what I must feel who was used to give. God only knows, and now to ask. Earl and Countess Nelson lived with me seven years. I educated Lady Charlotte, and paid at Eton for Trafalgar* [the honorary name given to Horace]. *I made Lord Nelson write the letter to Lord Sidmouth for the Prebendry of Canterbury, which his Lordship kindly gave him. They has never given the dear Horatia a frock or a sixpence.*[256]

Finding herself in yet further debt, Emma re-established contact with her old beau Sir Harry Fetherstonhaugh asking him for a loan of £500; *Pray let us meet . . . Let me come to Up Park* [sic] *for a few days to speak of old times . . . E. goes tonight but she is taken care of in case of any accident.*[257] The fact that she mentions her daughter Emma to him indicates that she thought him to be her father. He agreed to help her. The Boltons were sending food wherever they could – a couple of rabbits, a goose and a rib of pork but the creditors were pursuing Emma, while William Nelson constantly paid her annuity late. *That angel's last wishes all neglected, not to speak of the fraud that was acted to keep back the codicil . . . If I had any influenced over him, I used it to the good of my country . . . I have got all his letters, and near eight hundred of the Queen of Naples' letters, to show what I did for my King and Country, and prettily I am rewarded.*[258] Her financial situation was dire yet she was still giving presents to Nelson's relatives, sending a gown for Eliza Bolton, and a quilt for her sister Kate.

While Horatia remained at Merton with Mrs Cadogan, the surrounding land was sold off by Earl Nelson. Unable to pay the upkeep on her house in Clarges Street, and unwilling to give up a London residence altogether, Emma moved to a smaller, less salubrious residence at 136 Bond Street, sharing the drawing room with her landlady. In August, she went to stay with the Matchams who had just move into their new house at Ashfold in Sussex, accompanied by Horatia, Cecilia Connor, Lady Bolton with her daughter Anne, and various servants. The families then moved on to holiday at Worthing where they entertained themselves with donkey carts at the sea during the day, and in the evenings taking trips to the theatre. Her own side of the family, the Connors, Reynolds and Kidds continued to leech on Emma despite all the assistance she had already given them. Their neglect was remarked upon by Mrs Mari Thomas, the widow of her former employer, who sent her a letter 27 November 1807, 'I am truly sorry you have so much trouble with your relations and the ungrateful return your care and generosity meets with, indeed enough to turn your heart against them.'[259] Emma's uncle Thomas Kidd was a drunken lout who spent all the money she sent him in the alehouse; her nephew, Charles Connor was mad and by 1806 his sister, Ann, was quickly going the same way, declaring herself to be Emma's daughter. Meanwhile, Emma was still helping Nelson's relatives, trying to get the Matchams' and Boltons' names changed to 'Nelson' in order they might receive a pension, again via her friend Mr Rose. She also requested posts for Tom Bolton Junior at Cambridge and for Frederick Newcombe, another of her relatives who had been pursuer to Nelson.

By 1808, Merton was up for sale. Her neighbour Abraham Goldsmid brought together some city friends in November in a bid to help Emma and a group of trustees was set up to try and reverse Emma's financial decline. Further grief followed as William and Sarah Nelson's 19-year-old son Horatio (his name now altered to reflect his uncle's glory) died of typhoid fever; Kitty Matcham's 12-year-old son Francis, also died from a bowel problem. Her old friend Maria Carolina seemed unwilling to help Emma despite the efforts she had made to save the Queen's life in Naples. Emma turned to Lord St Vincent to enlist his help pressurising ministers to provide her with a pension.[260] Her old friend Rose also became involved in asking Lord Abercorn's assistance. She informed him, *I have been reduced to a situation the most painful as that can be conceived, and should have been actually confined in prison, if a few friends from attachments to the memory of Lord Nelson had not interfered to prevent it, under whose kind protection alone I am enabled to exist.*[261] She reminded him of the services that she had undertaken on behalf of her country and that she had never received any reward; she had hoped she would not need to claim it but she was now in the utmost need. Some ministers accepted her claim. Canning thought she richly deserved a pension but pointed to 'insurmountable difficulties'.[262] Even Greville supported her claims. But all of them prevaricated, saying it was due to the amount of time which had elapsed since the incidents. In truth, the real reason for her refusal was Hamilton's decision to marry Emma, and the scandal attached to her name, both because of her affairs prior to her marriage and because of her affair with Nelson.

Seeing her sunk so low, the old Duke of Queensberry took it upon himself to provide her with one of his properties, Heron Court in Richmond, and settled some of her debts to the tune of £2,500. Emma had contacted him in the hope he might buy Merton and allow her to live there but he had declined the offer. He was in his eighties and his philandering days were long since over but he was fond of Emma, had long looked upon Nelson as a friend, was a relative of Hamilton, and was only too pleased to help her out. She occasionally went to dances with 'old Q' and the Abercorns. In the summer of 1808, Emma and Horatia moved to Heron Court on the banks of the Thames. Emma was now ageing and fat, entertaining a bunch of coarse hangers-on who flattered her in exchange for food and drink. Imbibing excessively herself, she grew dissipated and an air of vulgarity descended on her soirées. According to George Matcham who visited Heron Court, 'where formerly elegance presided, vulgarity and grossièreté was now introduced. I could have almost wept at the change.' Even so, his mother was blatantly encouraging Emma to associate more closely with Old Q; 'I am glad you treated the old Duke with a sight of you in all your brilliancey. Depend upon it, it will be a thousand pounds in your pocket'.[263] Emma was putting her hopes on the old Duke dying and leaving her an inheritance or an annuity of some kind.

Unable to afford the upkeep on such a large house at Heron Court, with creditors encroaching, she was left with no option but to return to London with her mother and daughter to lodgings even worse than before. Ill-health descended on the family; Horatia suffered from a recurring unspecified illness possibly connected to her nerves which had started earlier in the summer, Emma contracted jaundice (no doubt a result of liver failure due to her drinking), and Mrs Cadogan suffered from chronic bronchitis. The Italian air had kept her condition at bay but with her return to London, the fog exacerbated it and she died on 14 January 1810. She had been the one person who had been with Emma throughout the whole of her life; she had become the loyal and trustworthy friend of both Nelson and Hamilton; and King Ferdinand had called her an angel for her services during their escape from Naples. She was buried in St Mary's Paddington, the same church where Emma had married Sir William 18 years earlier. Sir Harry Fetherstonhaugh wrote to commiserate with Emma, ' I trust you will soon be relieved from all that load of anxiety you have had so much lately, & which no one so little deserves.'[264] Emma, a year, on was still grieving, with *no pleasure but that of thinking and speaking of her.*[265] A further blow was the death of two more friends the same year; Goldsmid, who had helped sort out her finances and bought Merton from her, committed suicide; and her servant Fatima went mad and died in a lunatic asylum. Greville had already died the previous year on 23 April 1809. His efforts to ensnare a rich wife had come to nothing and he ended his life a bachelor. His estate passed into the hands of Fulke Greville and Emma's allowance of £800 per year from Hamilton's estate dried up on the grounds that she had borrowed against it.

Once Merton was sold, Emma and Horatia began a nomadic existence. They left Richmond in 1810, moved from Albemarle Street to 76 Piccadilly (above Bridgman's Confectioners) and on to Dover Street and then back to two different sets of lodgings in Bond Street. After her friends had sorted out her finances, Emma's assets were worth £17,500; her debt amounted to £8,000 raising to £10,000 with the interest owing to moneylenders. She was left with £900 per year including Horatia's annuity which should have been enough for them both to live comfortably. However, the monies owed to her were never all forthcoming, leading her into a round of chasing money and avoiding debt collectors. Yet she was still doling out money to her relatives and giving presents; in December, Anne Bolton wrote to her thanking her for a brooch and a gown. On his death on 23 December 1810, Queensberry did not forget Emma, leaving her £500 a year but due to legal wrangling on the part of Queensberry's relatives, she never saw any of this annuity either. It was thought he was worth around £900,000 when he died.

Writing in 1810, while living with her guardian Mrs Denis, Emma's first daughter forwarded a last letter to her mother. 'It might have been happy for me to have forgotten the past, and to have begun a new life with new ideas; but for my misfortune, my memory traces back circumstances which have taught me too much, yet not quite all I could have wished to have known – with you that resides, and ample reasons, no doubt, you have for not imparting them to me. Had you felt at liberty so to have done, I might have become reconciled to my former situation, and have been relieved as I then stood, for I had nothing to support me but the affection I bore you; on the other hand, doubts and fears but turns oppressed me, and I determined to rely only own efforts, rather than to submit to abject dependence, without a permanent name or acknowledged parents . . . But the time may come when the reasons may cease to operate, and then, with a heart filled with tenderness and affection, will I show you both duty and attachment'.[266] Despite such an emotional plea, Emma would never recognise her as her daughter, a dreadful blow for the young woman who had strong feelings towards Emma. Rejected, Emma's daughter went to live abroad, continuing in 'the painful employment' of governess and never saw or wrote to her mother again.

A great deal of confusion exists about who exactly Emma or Anna 'Carew' was – her first daughter who had changed her name, or her insane niece (as Emma claimed). She wrote in her will, *I do not leave anything to Ann or Mary Ann Connor, the daughter of Michael and Sarah Connor, as she has been wicked storytelling young woman, and tried to defame her best friends and relatives*, as she was claiming she was Emma's daughter. We know that there were two nieces on the Connor side, one called Ann and one called Mary, so it might have been either of them. In any case, Emma's will dated Merton 7 October 1806 left her daughter Emma without provision. She left a £100 annuity to her cousins Sarah and £50 to Cecilia but in her later will, as she developed increasing animosity towards her family, left them out. In her later will of 16 October 1808, she emphatically denied the claims of Ann Carew: *I declare before God, and as I hope to see Nelson in heaven, that Ann Connor, who goes by the name of Carew and tells many falsehoods that she is my daughter, but from what motive I know not, I declare that she is the eldest daughter of my mother's sister, Sarah Connor, and that I have the mother and six children to keep, all of them except two having turned out bad. I therefore beg of my mother to be kind to the two good ones, Sarah and Cecilia. This family having by their extravagance almost ruined me, I have nothing to leave them, and pray to god, to turn Ann Connor alias Carew's heart. I forgive her, but as there in madness in the Connor family, I hope it is only the effect of this disorder that may have induced this bad young woman to have persecuted me by her slander and falsehood.*[267]

In 1811, Emma borrowed £100 from Matcham, only to spend it on celebrating her 46th birthday at the Ship Inn, Greenwich Park. She was generally taking less care of herself but made an effort to make herself presentable for the wedding of Nelson's niece, Eliza Bolton. Despite all that Emma had given her while under her protection, Cecilia Connor forwarded a bill for Horatia's education. It would seem there had been a falling-out as Emma had refused to provide her with a character reference. The Boltons and Matchams invited Emma to stay but she was now increasingly withdrawing from her friends and family, and declined their well-intentioned offers. With debtors on all sides, she went to spend Christmas of 1812 in hiding with her old friend the opera singer Mrs Elizabeth Billington at her house in Bolton Row, Fulham where the unfortunate Horatia caught whooping cough.

Having sunk deeper into debt, at New Year 1813, Emma and 12-year-old Horatia found themselves in a debtor's prison. Not quite at the bottom of the pile, they managed to find a sponging house at 12 Temple Place within the rules of the King Bench. Those left with some money might escape gaol by renting out rooms within a certain designated area outside the prison walls. They were not allowed out but could receive visitors and were allowed to send out for things. At least here she was safe from other debtors since inmates could only be prosecuted for one debt at a time. Emma and Horatia also had a new companion with them, a Miss Wheatly, as well as their old faithful servant Dame Francis, all for whom she had to pay extra. The Boltons sent her food, as did the Matchams. For some time, both families appear to have been unaware that she was living in a sponging-house confined within the rules of the Kings Bench, as the Matchams invited her to Ashfold and the Boltons called at her home in Bond Street three times in May trying to see her. Emma turned to Mr

James Perry, future editor of the *Morning Chronicle*, for help. He showed himself to be a true friend to Emma, raising money to bail her out. Joshua Jonathan Smith, Alderman of the City, also came to her aid, buying her furniture at Richmond for £400 as well as Nelson's bloodied uniform, most painful for her to part with. For a time she was back in her rooms in Bond Street but it was not long before she was to return to debtor's prison.

Emma now made yet another attempt at trying to obtain money from the government in two memorials one to the Prince Regent, the other to the King again requesting recognition of her services in the form of a pension. To the King, she wrote on March 1813 *[I] had an opportunity of obtaining, and actually did obtain, the King of Spain's letter to the King of Naples expressive of its intention to declare war on England. This important document, your Majesty's memorialist delivered to her husband, Sir William Hamilton, who immediately transmitted it to your Majesty's Ministers.*[268] So why did she never receive any pension or reward from the British government for her services? Hamilton received a pension as did Nelson for his role in the events, so it seems that Emma was ignored because she was a woman. Even Nelsons' wife received a pension after his death merely for being married to a hero. There is therefore reason to presume that the lack of financial reward coming from the government to Emma, even as Hamilton's wife, was mainly due to her reputation and sexual history.

Arguments were regularly occurring between Emma and Horatia – Emma, now 48, had become increasingly short-tempered, was drinking too much, and frequently became aggressive. On top of this, Horatia was developing her own personality and showing signs of rebelliousness; continually on the move, missing her world at Merton as well as the relatives she had been surrounded with while growing up, it was unsurprising she was unhappy and depressed. She was also showing her mother's high spirits, for Emma told her *I grieve and lament at your turbulent*

*passions . . . Listen to a kind, good mother who has ever been to you affec-
tionate, truly kind and who had nether spared pains nor expense to make
you the most amiable and most accomplish'd of your sex. Ah, Horatia! If
you had grown up as I wish'd you, what a joy, what a comfort might you
have been to me! . . . Reform your conduct, or you will be detested by all
the world, and when you shall no longer have my fostering arm to sheild
you, woe betide you, you will sink to nothing. Be good, be honourable, tell
not falsehoods, be not capricious.*[269] Emma threatened to pack her off
to school unless she reformed. Yet Emma had sold off Horatia's
favourite silver cup, a gift from her father, to a Bond Street
silversmith to pay off her debts and Horatia was entitled to feel
some resentment at finding herself in a predicament not of her
own making. Even now, despite what she said in her letters to
Horatia, Emma was denying she was her mother, merely telling
Horatia that her mother was *too great a lady to be mentioned.*[270] But
Mrs Bolton had also used the same words about Emma so the
connection was all too obvious.

Rearrested, this time for her debts to a coach builder, on 13
July, Emma was back in Temple Place where she was held for nine
months. Her remaining worldly goods at Bond Street were all
sold off by order of the Sheriff in order to pay off her creditors; two
of Nelson's sea chests, the remains of Hamilton's rare books,
Horatia's doll's bed, a four-poster mahogany bed, a piano, her
writing desk, dressing table, Grecian couch; all her glass and
china; her valuables – her diamond watch, a gold box presented
to Nelson in 1802; and even all her books and magazines. Again
James Perry and Alderman Smith stepped in to purchase the
most important relics to prevent them being lost forever. Smith
packed them away in crates and stored them in a warehouse
in Southwark. The Matchams still offered their friendship and
sent her £100 but Emma suffered a further blow when she
received the news of Susannah Bolton's death in August 1813.
While selling off the rest of their memorabilia and the gifts

Nelson had given Horatia, Emma continued to entertain. Sir Thomas Lewis called on her to drink a toast to Nelson on the anniversary of the Battle of the Nile. She was also visited by the Linds, the Denises. Mrs Billington, Mr Perry, the Duke of Sussex, Colonel Smith and O'Kelly and the singer Anna Storace for Horatia's birthday. Royalty was still visiting Emma even in the sponging house; on Christmas Day 1813, they held a final party. The Duke of Sussex with his mistress Mrs Bugge and Sir William Dillon were among the guests. Dillon recalled the celebrations in his diary – the table laid with rented silver plate but lacking a carving knife, and he jokingly suggested he pluck at the bird with his fingers. Alderman Smith paid the bills at her sponging house, and once again, bailed her out. Mr Matcham wrote offering potatoes, a turkey and anything their farm could supply.

April 1814 saw Napoleon's abdication and celebrations in the streets. Around the same time, *Letters of Lord Nelson to Lady Hamilton* was published. Emma had allowed hack and bookseller James Harrison access to her letters in order to write the biography of Nelson, *Life of Lord Nelson*, published in 1806. Nelson's wife, Fanny was unfairly castigated in the book, probably in obeisance to Emma. Now Emma claimed Harrison had somehow, by deception, obtained the letters of a more personal nature not intended for publication. Emma denied all knowledge of any connection to the book and wrote to the newspapers from Calais, *I know nothing of these infamous publications that are imputed to me. My letters were stolen from me by that scoundrel whose family I had in charity so long supported. I never once saw or knew of them.*[271] The letters concerning the Prince of Wales were inflammatory particularly the parts where Nelson had referred to him as a 'villain' and an 'unprincipled liar', and ruined any slight chance she might have of ever obtaining a pension. She claimed Nelson's handwriting had been forged but they were genuine.

With the war at an end and the continent opening up, many

people were taking trips abroad. George Matcham wrote to Emma inviting them both to join his family as they prepared to start a life elsewhere. They offered to take care of both Emma and Horatia but Emma was too proud. In any case, with debtors still hovering to pounce, she had to move quicker than the Matchams were able (the Matchams did not go abroad until 1818) once she was allowed to leave the sponging house. She wrote to Earl Nelson asking him for some money she was due from the Bronte estate, and he sent her £225. She also contacted Mr Perry who managed to raise more money through a collection in the City and assisted paying off the rest of her debts and she was finally let out. As soon as she was released, she took passage with Horatia on *The Little Tom* from London Bridge Wharf in June 1814 setting sail for Calais. Having retained £50 for herself, she went directly to the most lavish inn, Dessein's. Inevitably, their money ran out and they soon they had to move to the less fashionable Quillac's. Horatia

Emma's final refuge the port of Calais, a drawing from 1829

began attending a day school in the morning, where she was learning harp, piano and languages. Emma boasted *Horatia is improving in person and education every day. She speaks French like a French girl, Italian, German English, etc.*[272] They would meet at one, dine at three, then walk out in the evening together.

Within a couple of months, they were obliged to move out of the town into a village farmhouse a few miles away at Saint-Pierre where her old companion Dame Francis joined them. They soon moved again to another place nearby with large rooms and huge garden where they could live more cheaply until Horatia's interest on her inheritance came through on her 'birthday' on 29 October. Emma wrote to Earl Nelson requesting her Bronte annuity be paid quarterly instead of half-yearly but he replied he was too poor. With the money running out, she then wrote to Robert Fulke Greville for the annuity he owed from the conditions of Hamilton's will. He responded that the money was owed to her creditors and he had been advised by his legal advisors not to pay out until the matter was sorted.

Emma had been ill for eight months with jaundice, an effect of her heavy drinking. Increasingly desperate for money, on 7 October Emma appealed to the Home Secretary Lord Sidmouth for relief on behalf of Horatia for *services to my country . . . Let Horatia, who will be fourteen on October 29, finish her education, let her be provided for. At present we have not one shilling in our pockets, although I spent all I had on Earl Nelson.*[273] After a letter from Horatia, Earl Nelson reluctantly sent £10 and a friend another £20. Emma and Horatio left the farmhouse and took up smaller lodgings in the Rue Française, pawning what they had left in order to live. Recognising the extreme difficulty they were in, Horatia wrote to Mr Matcham who instructed her to find someone to look after Emma and come home immediately, an impossible mission given they had no money. Nor could Horatia merely desert Emma who was now continually drunk, abusive and never left her bed. She was to write about her mother, 'For some time before her death she was not kind to me, but she had much to try her.'[274]

Emma finally died, a broken woman, on 15 January 1815. She had asked in her will to be buried in St Paul's near Nelson. According to Emma, the three of them had wanted to be buried near to each other; *If the King [had] granted him a public funeral, this would have been, that three persons who were so much attached to each other from virtue and friendship should have been laid in one grave when they quitted this ill-natured slanderous world.* She attacked the government for refusing to recognise her services; *I have done my King & Country some service but as they were ungrateful enough to neglect the request of the virtuous Nelson in providing for me, I do not expect they will do anything for his child.*[275] This was not to be and she was buried alone in a foreign country.

The British Consul, Mr Henry Cadogan financed the funeral – an oak coffin, shroud and candles for a Catholic Mass totalling £28 10s but it was her last friend, Alderman Smith, who reimbursed the expenses. Naval officers at Calais followed the hearse. Emma had made a second will in September 1811 leaving everything to Horatia. Surprisingly, if Horatia was to die intestate everything was to go to Mr John and Amy Moore, Emma's maternal aunt and uncle of whom we heard little throughout her life. Horatia at last could make her way to Ashfold to be taken care of by the Matchams, Mr Matcham having hurried to Dover to pick her up. In 1822, Horatia married a vicar, the Reverend Philip Ward, bearing him 10 children and lived a long life, dying at the age of 80 in 1881. Although she accepted her father was Nelson, Horatia always refused to believe Emma was her mother.

Emma's Legacy

In a time when worldly exploits were thought to be the prerogative of men, Emma serves as an example of a woman who managed to forge her own destiny in a man's world. Her refusal to be controlled was shown in her frequent outbursts of temper, a trait she eventually managed to subdue to her own advantage. In her early days, she taught herself to be attentive to men and to restrain her behaviour in order to secure her position. Having had the misfortune to fall pregnant after revelling in the high life, she managed to extricate herself from a dire situation, to secure not only her own welfare but that of her whole family, including finding homes for her mother and daughter. She set about creating her own legend, first as a member of the aristocracy, entertaining the *beau monde*, then as a diplomat and spy at Naples. Her continual letters to ministers, the Prince of Wales and the King show her desperate desire not merely for money, but for recognition.

Emma was grateful to Hamilton for loving her and marrying her. He raised her from the subservience she had experienced for so long with Greville. Recognising the power of education, she soaked up everything on offer, her ability for languages proving a valuable asset for Nelson as a translator. But it was Nelson who was her passion, her soulmate, her unconditional love. They were alike in that both of them needed admiration; both wanted fame and glory. It was this love, however, that cost her all she had gained by her marriage to Sir William.

Emma's attempts to manipulate her own history and turn herself into a heroine have, to a large extent, been the reason that

Joseph Nolleken's bust of the young Emma

her importance in history has been overlooked. Her over-dramatisation of events led people to believe that she had actually achieved little. Yet she played a significant role in assisting her country during the French Revolutionary War, working alongside both Nelson and Hamilton, intercepting vital letters, interceding with the Queen to allow the British fleet entry into Sicilian ports and conveyed information to the British government. Was it because she was a woman that her role in these incidents is ignored and that her beauty and sexuality is emphasised? Certainly, much more was made of her Attitudes than Sir Williams's violin playing, yet her life was in as much danger as Nelson's when she helped in the escape from Naples.

Emma's loyalty and perseverance make her an admirable character but her high sense of drama and her theatricality allowed her detractors to divert attention from her real abilities. She was naturally adventurous, stood firm in adversity and was often at her best in a crisis. Although some have argued that Emma exaggerated her political importance, neither Nelson nor Hamilton thought she did, both writing to the King and government ministers requesting a pension for her work at Naples; even Greville did so.

Notes

MS = Manuscript
*Where possible in the references I have
indicated the date after the source.*

1. Brian Fothergill, *Sir William
   Hamilton. Envoy Extraordinary*
   (Faber & Faber, London: 1969),
   p 219.
2. Anon, *The Letters of Lord Nelson to
   Lady Hamilton; with supplement of
   interesting letters by distinguished
   characters* (Thomas Lovewell & Co,
   London: 1814), Vol I, p 135, 26
   August 1803; Walter Sichel,
   Emma Lady Hamilton (Archibald
   Constable, London: 1905), p 28,
   hereafter Sichel, *Emma*.
3. Egerton MS 1623 f 32, 2 April
   1802.
4. Add. MSS 34989 f 24.
5. John Cordy Jeaffreson, *Beaux and
   Belles of England. Lady Hamilton and
   Lord Nelson*, Vol I and II
   (Athenaeum Press, London: 1897).
   See Eirlys Gruffyd, 'Lord Nelson's
   Emma', *Buckley: The Magazine of the
   Buckley Society*, No 19 (Spring
   1995); G I Hawkes, 'Emma, Lady
   Hamilton. Her Family and Friends
   on Deeside', *Buckley: The Magazine
   of the Buckley Society*, No 21 (Spring
   1997). My thanks to Simon Gotts,
   Information Librarian at Flintshire
   Library and Information Service,
   County Hall for providing me with
   copies of the requested information.
6. Thomas Pettigrew, *Memoirs of the
   Life of Vice-Admiral Lord Viscount
   Nelson* (T & W Boone, London:
   1849), p 465.
7. Morrison MS 983, 17 November
   1809.
8. Morrison MS 959, 16 October
   1808.
9. Westminster City Archives.
10. *Brief Description of the cities of
    London & Westminster* (London:
    1776), p 17.
11. Dorothy George, *London Life in the
    Eighteenth Century* (1925; reprinted
    Penguin, London: 1965), p 119.
12. Fothergill, *Sir William Hamilton*,
    p 252.
13. J Hanway, *The Defects of Police in
    the Cause of Immorality, and the
    Continual Robberies Committed,
    Particularly in and about the
    Metropolis* (London: 1775), p 12.
14. Morrison MS 113, 10 January
    1782.
15. Morrison MS 114, 10 January
    1782.
16. Morrison MS 156, November
    1786.
17. Morrison MS 114, 10 January
    1782.
18. Vivien Jones (ed), *Women in the
    Eighteenth Century. Constructions of
    Femininity* (Routledge, London:
    1990), p 45.
19. Pettigrew, *Memoirs of Nelson*, Vol
    II, pp 596–7, 17 May 1804.
20. Morrison MS 199, 20 December
    1791.
21. Morrison MS 125, 15 June 1784.
22. Morrison MS 124, 12 June 1784.
23. Morrison MS 126, 22 June 1784.
24. Add. MSS 42071 f 4, 1 June
    1785.
25. Morrison MS 126, 22 June 1784.

26. Morrison MS 136; 10 March 1785.

27. Morrison MS 137, 5 May 1785.

28. Morrison MS 137, 5 May 1785.

29. Add. MSS 42071 ff 5-6, 1 June 1785.

30. Morrison MS 142, 2 December 1785.

31. Morrison MS 144, 20 January 1786.

32. Morrison MS 156, November 1786.

33. Morrison MS 149, 25 April 1786.

34. Johann Wolfgang von Goethe, *Italian Journey 1786-1788*, tr W H Auden and Elizabeth Mayer (Collins, London: 1962), p 207.

35. Goethe, *Italian Journey*, p 211.

36. Fothergill, *Sir William Hamilton*, p 61 quoting *Pembroke Papers*, Vol I, p 225

37. Percy A Scholes (ed), Charles Burney, *Musical Tours in Italy* (London: 1959), Vol I, pp 264–7.

38. Morrison MS 150, 30 April 1786.

39. Fothergill, *Sir William Hamilton*, p 58.

40. Morrison MS 152, 22 July 1786.

41. Egerton MS 2634 f 93.

42. Julie Peakman, *Mighty Lewd Books. The Development of Pornography in Eighteenth Century England* (Palgrave, London: 2003), pp 109–11.

43. Illchester, Earl of (ed), *Journal of Elizabeth, Lady Holland* (London: 1908), Vol II, p 9.

44. Morrison MS 152, 22 July 1786.

45. Morrison MS 153, 1 August 1786.

46. Morrison MS 153, 1 August 1786.

47. Morrison MS 152, 22 July 1786.

48. Henry Swinburne, *The Court of Europe at the Close of the Last Century* (London: 1895), Vol I, p 32.

49. Madame Le Brun, *Memoirs of Madame Vigeé Lebrun* (Grant Richards, London: 1904), p 72.

50. E and F Anson (eds), *Mary Hamilton* (London: 1925), p 146.

51. Morrison MS 157, 26 December 1786.

52. Morrison MS 159, 8 January 1786.

53. Morrison MS 157, 26 December 1786.

54. Morrison MS 164.

55. Add. MSS 34048 f 30, 4 July 1786.

56. Add. MSS 34048 f 33, 26 September 1786.

57. Morrison MS 165, 16 February 1787.

58. Morrison MS 164.

59. Sichel, *Emma*, p 100 quoting from an unpublished letter of 17 May 1804, in Sotheby's catalogue June 1905.

60. Goethe, *Italian Journey*, pp 199–212.

61. Sir Gilbert Elliot, *Life and Letters of First Earl of Minto* (London: 1874), Vol I, p 406.

62. Morrison MS 168, 4 August 1787.

63. Goethe, *Italian Journey*, p 220.

64. Illchester (ed), *Journal of Elizabeth, Lady Holland*, Vol I, p 243.

65. Illchester (ed), *Journal of Elizabeth, Lady Holland*, Vol I, p 242.

66. Morrison MS 250, 18 December 1794.

67. Elliot, *Life and Letters of First Earl of Minto*, Vol I, p 401.

68. Morrison MS 160, 10 January 1787.

69. Morrison MS 168, 4 August 1787.

70. Morrison MS 163, 18 January 1787.

71. Morrison MS 168, 4 August 1787.

72. Elliot, *Life and Letters of First Earl of Minto*, Vol II, p 364.

73. Morrison MS 189, January 1791.

74. Add. MSS 34048 ff 61-2, 6 April 1790.

75. Morrison MS 177, 26 May 1789.

76. Morrison MS 185, 21 September 1790.

77. Morrison MS 189, January 1791; Anon, *The Letters of Lord Nelson to Lady Hamilton*, Vol II, p 174, 18 January 1792.

78. Morrison MS 190, 8 March 1791.

79. Add. MSS 34048, f 61.

80. Morrison MS 189, January 1791.
81. See letters in William Hayley, *The Life of George Romney* (T Payne, London: 1809), pp 119, 158–9.
82. Hayley, *Life of Romney*, pp 158, 165.
83. Hugh Tours, *The Life and Letters of Emma Hamilton* (V. Gollancz, London: 1963), p 90.
84. Sichel, *Emma*, p 137.
85. Morrison MS 200, 1791.
86. Brian Connell, *Portrait of a Whig Peer* (Methuen and Co, London: 1910), p 276.
87. E and F Anson (eds), *Mary Hamilton*, p 317.
88. Elliot, *Life and Letters of First Earl of Minto*, Vol I, p 402.
89. Morrison MS 199, 20 December 1791.
90. Morrison MS 208, 17 April 1792.
91. Elliot, *Life and Letters of First Earl of Minto*, Vol I, p 406, 11 January 1792.
92. Egerton MS 2637 f 92.
93. Morrison MS 215, 4 December 1792.
94. Egerton MS 2636 f 261, 27 October 1778.
95. Egerton MS 2639 f 12, 10 March 1787.
96. Fothergill, *Sir William Hamilton*, p 264.
97. Anon, *Lord Nelson's Letters to Lady Hamilton*, Vol II, p 173
98. Morrison MS 221, 2 June 1793.
99. Tours, *The Life and Letters of Emma Hamilton*, p 107.
100. Morrison MS 221, 2 June 1793.
101. Morrison MS 250, 18 December 1794.
102. Pettigrew, *Memoirs of Nelson*, Vol I, p 40.
103. Mollie Hardwick, *Emma, Lady Hamilton* (Holt Rinehart and Winston: New York: 1969), p 49 citing MS in E Huntington Library, San Marino.
104. Add. MSS 34989 f 12, 3 October 1798.
105. Jeaffreson, *Lady Hamilton and Lord Nelson*, Vol I, p 294.

106. Morrison MS 226, 27 September 1793.
107. Pettigrew, *Memoirs of Nelson*, Vol I, p 42.
108. Fothergill, *Sir William Hamilton*, p 280.
109. Morrison MS 250, 18 December 1794.
110. Elliot, *Life and Letters of First Earl of Minto*, Vol II, p 364.
111. Egerton MS 1615 f 18, 17 April 1795.
112. Morrison MS 263, 19 April 1795.
113. Egerton MS 1615 ff 20-22, 17 April 1795.
114. Morrison MS 263, 19 April 1795.
115. Morrison MS 1046, March 1813.
116. Morrison MS 274, February 1796.
117. Add. MSS 34710 f 23, 17 November 1795.
118. Morrison MS 201, 10 January 1792.
119. Morrison MS 285, August 1796.
120. Morrison MS 282, 7 June 1796.
121. Morrison MS 287, 21 September 1796.
122. Morrison MS 290, 1 December 1796.
123. Egerton MS 1615 ff 8, 69, 4 June 1795, 3 December 1796.
124. Anon, *The Letters of Lord Nelson to Lady Hamilton,* Vol II, p 188.
125. Anon, *The Letters of Lord Nelson to Lady Hamilton*, Vol I, p 181.
126. Pettigrew, *Memoirs of Nelson*, Vol I, p 119.
127. Add. MSS 34989 f 3, 8 September 1798.
128. Geoffrey Rawston (ed), *Nelson's Letters* (J M Dent, London: 1960), p 182, 17 June 1798.
129. Morrison MS 320, 18 June 1798.
130. O A Sherrard, *A Life of Emma Hamilton* (Sidgewick & Jackson, London: 1927), p 186.
131. Letter from Nelson to Fanny, 16 September 1798 in Clement Dane (ed), *The Nelson Touch. An Anthology of Lord Nelson's Letters* (William Heinemann, London: 1942), p 85.

132. Add. MSS 34,989 f 4, 8 September 1798.

133. Hibbert, *Nelson*, p 151.

134. Add. MSS 34989 f 8-10, 2 December 1798.

135. Pettigrew, *Memoirs of Nelson*, Vol I, p 140.

136. Cornelia Knight, *Autobiography* (W H Allen, London: 1861), pp 111–14.

137. Pettigrew, *Memoirs of Nelson*, Vol I, p 150, 25 September 1798.

138. Egerton MS 1615 ff 63, 117.

139. Hibbert, *Nelson*, p 152.

140. Add MS 34989 f 8, 2 October 1798.

141. Rawston (ed), *Nelson's Letters*, p 201, 4 October 1798.

142. Add. MSS 34989 f 23, 27 October 1798.

143. Add. MSS 34989 f 15, 20 October 1798.

144. Egerton MS 1616 f 38.

145. Morrison MS 370, 7 January 1799.

146. Hibbert, *Nelson*, p 172.

147. Morrison MS 370, 7 January 1799.

148. Morrison MS 369, 6 January 1799.

149. Morrison MS 396, 8 June 1799.

150. Hardwick, *Emma, Lady Hamilton*, p 62.

151. Tours, *Life and Letters of Emma Hamilton*, p 144.

152. Sichel, *Emma*, p 280.

153. Anon, *The Letters of Lord Nelson to Lady Hamilton*, Vol I, p 9.

154. Morrison MS 391, 25 May 1799.

155. Morrison MS 369, 6 January 1799.

156. Morrison MS 411, 19 July 1799.

157. Fothergill, *Sir William Hamilton*, p 359.

158. Sichel, *Emma*, p 303.

159. Illchester (ed), *Journal of Lady Holland*, Vol II, pp 12–13.

160. Morrison MS 408, 17 July 1799.

161. Morrison MS 411, 19 July 1799.

162. Morrison MS 381, 8 April 1799.

163. Sichel, *Emma*, p 284.

164. N H Grant, *The Letters of Mary Nisbet of Dirleton, Countess of Elgin* (London: 1926), p 17.

165. George P B Naish, *Nelson's Letters to his Wife and Other Documents 1785–1831* (Routledge & Kegan Paul, London: 1958), p 565.

166. Hibbert, *Nelson*, p 176, 29 January 1800.

167. Morrison MS 516, 17 February 1801.

168. Anon, *The Letters of Lord Nelson to Lady Hamilton*, Vol I, p 269.

169. Edgar Vincent, *Nelson: Love & Fame* (Yale University Press, London & New Haven: 2003), p 212, 24 October 1799.

170. Anon, *The Letters of Lord Nelson to Lady Hamilton*, Vol I, p 277.

171. Sichel, *Emma*, pp 328–30.

172. Tours, *Life and Letters of Emma Hamilton*, p 151.

173. Knight, *Autobiography*, Vol I, pp 319–23; Elliot, *Life and Letters of First Earl of Minto*, Vol III, p 147.

174. Roger Hudson (ed), *Nelson and Emma* (The Folio Society, London: 1994), p 163, 30 August 1800.

175. Elliot, *Life and Letters of First Earl of Minto*, Vol III, p 114, 23 March 1800.

176. Sichel, *Emma*, p 332.

177. Anon, *The Letters of Lord Nelson to Lady Hamilton*, Vol I, p 272.

178. Tours, *Life and Letters of Emma Hamilton*, p 156, 3 October 1800.

179. Morrison MS 497, 9 November 1800.

180. Sichel, *Emma*, p 335, 1 September 1800.

181. Connell, *Portrait of a Whig Peer*, p 436.

182. Connell, *Portrait of a Whig Peer*, p 436.

183. Sichel, *Emma*, p 340.

184. W H Long, *Memoirs of Emma, Lady Hamilton* (Gibbings & Co, London: 1899), pp 263–3.

185. Hibbert, *Nelson*, p 227; NMM, CRK 19/249, 15 October 1801.

186. Pettigrew, *Memoirs of Nelson*, Vol I, p 405.
187. Add. MSS 42071 f 5-6, 1 June 1785.
188. Naish, *Nelson's Letters to his Wife*, p 577, 20 February 1801.
189. Hardwick, *Emma, Lady Hamilton*, pp 88–9.
190. Morrison MS 504, 1 February 1801.
191. Morrison MS 505, 3 February 1801.
192. Morrison MS 513.
193. Morrison MS 518, 17 February 1801.
194. Morrison MS 520, 18 February 1801.
195. Anon, *The Letters of Lord Nelson to Lady Hamilton*, Vol II, p 200.
196. Morrison MS 531, 1 March 1801.
197. Morrison MS 539, 6 March 1801.
198. Morrison MS 528, 23 February 1801.
199. Morrison MS 539, 6 March 1801.
200. Morrison MS 532, 1 March 1801.
201. Add. MSS 34989 f 38, 24 February 1801.
202. Add. MSS 34989 f 42-3.
203. Morrison MS 502, 25 January 1801.
204. Add. MS 34989 f 38, 24 February 1801.
205. Naish, *Nelson's Letters to his Wife*, p 586.
206. Morrison MS 536, 4 March 1801.
207. Morrison MS 550, 31 March 1801.
208. Morrison MS 543, 11 March 1801.
209. Morrison MS 538, 547, 6 and 16 March 1801.
210. Sichel, *Emma*, pp 347–8.
211. Morrison MS 549, 21 March 1801.
212. Hibbert, *Nelson*, p 261.
213. Morrison MS 572, April 1801.
214. Morrison MS 621, end of September 1801.
215. Egerton MS 2240 f 106, 9 October 1801.
216. Sichel, *Emma*, p 379, citing Sotheby's catalogue 8 July 1905.
217. Anon, *The Letters of Lord Nelson to Lady Hamilton*, Vol I, p 102.
218. Add. MSS 34989 ff 51-52.
219. Sichel, *Emma*, p 374.
220. Elliot, *Life and Letters of First Earl of Minto*, Vol II, pp 242–3, 283.
221. Add MSS 42071 ff 21-22, 24 January 1802.
222. Anon, *The Letters of Lord Nelson to Lady Hamilton*, Vol II, p 220.
223. Egerton MS 2240 f 139.
224. NMM/NWD 9594/9.
225. Morrison MS 679, 680, August 1802.
226. Morrison MS 684, 1802.
227. Pettigrew, *Memoirs of Nelson*, Vol II, p 295.
228. Egerton MS 2240 f 157, 6 April 1803.
229. Pettigrew, *Memoirs of Nelson*, Vol II, p 322.
230. Egerton MS 2240 f 164.
231. Sichel, *Emma*, pp 401–2.
232. Anon, *The Letters of Lord Nelson to Lady Hamilton*, Vol II, pp 67–8, 30 August 1804.
233. Morrison MS 212, 16 May 1803.
234. Morrison MS 713, 20 May 1803.
235. Hardwick, *Emma, Lady Hamilton*, p 166.
236. Morrison MS 779, 13 August 1804.
237. Anon, *The Letters of Lord Nelson to Lady Hamilton*, Vol I, p 158, 18 October 1803.
238. Morrison MS 821, 18 July 1805.
239. Elliot, *Life and Letters of First Earl of Minto*, Vol III, p 363.
240. Long, *Memoirs of Lady Hamilton*, p 322.
241. Anon, *The Letters of Lord Nelson to Lady Hamilton*, Vol I, pp 176–7.
242. Sichel, *Emma*, p 10, 11 March 1804.
243. Hardwick, *Emma, Lady Hamilton*, p 195.
244. Sherrard, *Life of Emma Hamilton*, p 329.
245. Add. MSS 34992 f 3, 13 September 1805.
246. Morrison MS 849, 27 October 1804.

247. Morrison MS 845, 8 October 1805.

248. Morrison MS 848, 21 October 1805.

249. Morrison MS 847, 19 October 1805.

250. Tours, *Life and Letters of Emma Hamilton*, p 220.

251. George Rose, *Diaries and Correspondence of the Right Honourable George Rose* (Bentley, London: 1860), Vol I, p 241.

252. Facsimile of Lord Nelson's letter, 19 October 1805, Royal Naval Museum Library, Portsmouth.

253. Add. MSS 34,989 ff 55, 56, 14 November 1806.

254. Morrison MS 865, 13 February 1806; Morrison MS 874, 29 March 1806.

255. Add. MSS 34,992 f 103, 13 September 1806.

256. Sichel, *Emma*, p 437, Appendix Part II C10a, 12 September 1814.

257. Hardwick, *Emma, Lady Hamilton*, p 218, 2 July 1806.

258. Sichel, *Emma*, p 438.

259. Morrison MS 930, 27 November 1807.

260. Morrison MS 949, July 1808.

261. Sichel, *Emma*, p 446.

262. Morrison MS 948, 21 July 1808.

263. Hardwick, *Emma, Lady Hamilton*, p 235.

264. Morrison MS 989, 14 January 1810.

265. Sichel, *Emma*, p 511.

266. Morrison MS 1003, 1810.

267. Morrison MS 959, 16 October 1808.

268. Morrison MS 1045-6, March 1813.

269. Morrison MS 1047, 18 April 1813.

270. Sichel, *Emma*, p 460.

271. Sichel, *Emma*, p 462.

272. Morrison MS 1055, 21 September 1814.

273. Hardwick, *Emma, Lady Hamilton*, p 283.

274. Winifred Gérin, *Horatia Nelson* (Oxford University Press, Oxford & New York: 1970), p 207.

275. Morrison MS 959, 16 October 1808.

Chronology

Year	Age	Life
1765		26 April: Born. 12 May: Baptised.
1781	16	Summer spent at Uppark with Sir Harry Fetherstonhaugh.
1782	17	Birth of 'Little Emma', her first daughter. Moves in with Greville. First sits for Romney for sketches as 'Nature'.
1784	19	Meets Sir William Hamilton at Edgware Row.
1786	21	26 April: Arrives in Naples on her 21st birthday with her mother.
1787	22	Tours Italy with Sir William, visiting Sorrento, Ischia and Puglia.
1791	26	Returns to England with Sir William and her mother. 6 September: Marries Sir William.
1792	27	Increasingly involved with Queen Maria Carolina and matters at the Royal Court in Naples.

Year	History	Culture
1765	Parliament passes Stamp Act taxing American colonies. Launch of Nelson's future flagship HMS *Victory*.	Horace Walpole, *The Castle of Otranto*.
1781	British surrender at Yorktown ends American War of Independence.	Mozart, opera *Idomeno*.
1782	Spanish siege of Gibraltar lifted. James Watt invents double-acting steam engine.	Mozart, opera, *Die Entführung aus dem Serail*.
1784	First balloon ascent in England.	Sir Joshua Reynolds, painting 'Mrs Siddons as the Tragic Muse'.
1786	Death of Frederick the Great of Prussia.	Robert Burns, *Poems chiefly in the Scottish dialect*.
1787	Parlement of Paris demands Louis XVI summons the French Estates-General.	Mozart, opera *Don Giovanni*.
1791	Louis XVI and family captured at Varennes trying to flee France.	Boswell, *Life of Samuel Johnson*.
1792	French Republic proclaimed: Royal Family imprisoned. France declares war on Austria and Prussia.	Thomas Paine, *The Rights of Man*, Part 2.

Year	Age	Life
1793	28	June: The Hamiltons and the Royal Family move out to Caserta as the political situation in Naples deteriorates. 11 September: Nelson arrives in Naples and meets Emma and Sir William for the first time the following day.
1795	30	Emma intercepts secret letters from the King of Spain to his brother King Ferdinand of Naples.
1796	31	14 February: Battle of Cape St Vincent.
1798	33	Emma greets Nelson returning to Naples from success at the Battle of the Nile. 26 December: Arrive in Palermo fleeing political unrest in Naples.
1799	34	24 June: Emma, Nelson and Sir William return to Naples to reinstate the King. 8 August: The trio return to Palermo to celebrate their success.
1800	35	6 November: The trio arrive in England after Hamilton's recall from Naples. Christmas together at Fonthill.

Year	History	Culture
1793	Execution of Louis XVI. Britain and France at war.	Canova, sculpture 'Cupid and Psyche'.
1795	Napoleon Bonaparte appointed to command French army in Italy.	Goya, portrait 'The Duchess of Alba'.
1796	Bonaparte defeats the Austrians at Lodi and Arcoli: enters Milan. Spain declares war on Britain.	Wordsworth, *The Borderers*.
1798	French capture Rome. The Battle of the Pyramids: Bonaparte's army defeats the Mamelukes in Egypt.	Wordsworth and Coleridge, *Lyrical Ballads*.
1799	Bonaparte defeated at Acre: returns to France and becomes Consul. Russians defeat French in northern Italy.	Haydn, oratorio *The Creation*.
1800	Bonaparte, now First Consul, defeats the Austrians at Marengo. British capture Malta.	Schiller, play *Mary Stuart*.

Year	Age	Life
1801	36	29 January: Birth of Horatia. July: The trio set out on a three-month tour of Wales. October: Emma purchases Merton on Nelson's behalf.
1803	38	6 April: Death of Sir William Hamilton.
1804	39	Birth of third daughter, also named Emma. She died soon after.
1805	40	21 October: Nelson killed at the Battle of Trafalgar.
1808	43	Summer: Moves into Heron Court, the Duke of Queensbury's Richmond property.
1809	44	Merton sold to pay off her debts. 23 April: Death of Greville.
1810	45	Mother dies. Emma and Horatia on the move, taking lodgings in Albemarle St, Piccadilly, Dover St and Bond St over the next few years.

Year	History	Culture
1801	Battle of Copenhagen. British defeat French in Egypt.	David, painting 'Napoléon à Grand Saint-Bernard'
1803	War breaks out again between Britain and France after collapse of Peace of Amiens.	Turner, painting 'Calais Pier'.
1804	Bonaparte crowns himself Emperor Napoleon I. Spain declares war on Britain.	Beethoven, symphony *Eroica*.
1805	Battle of Austerlitz. Peace of Pressburg between Austria and France.	Beethoven, opera *Fidelio*.
1808	French invade Spain: Joseph Bonaparte made king.	Goethe, *Faust* Part I.
1809	Peninsula War: Sir Arthur Wellesley made Duke of Wellington for victories at Talavera and Albuera.	Beethoven, *Emperor* concerto.
1810	Napoleon marries Archduchess Marie Louise of Austria.	Goya, painting 'Los Desastres de la Guerra'.

Year	Age	Life
1813	48	Emma in debtors' prison.
1814	49	Publication of Letters of Lord Nelson to Lady Hamilton. June: Emma and Horatia leave England for Calais.
1815	50	15 January: Death of Emma.

Year	History	Culture
1813	Napoleon defeated at Battle of Leipzig. Peninsula War: Wellington defeats French at Vittoria and enters France.	Jane Austen, *Pride and Prejudice*.
1814	Napoleon abdicates and is exiled to Elba. Congress of Vienna opens.	Jane Austen, *Mansfield Park*. Dulwich Picture Gallery opens.
1815	The Hundred Days: Napoleon returns from Elba but is defeated at Waterloo: abdicates again and exiled to St Helena.	Nash rebuilds Brighton Pavilion in pseudo-oriental style.

Bibliography

Primary Sources

NB: The best primary sources are the original manuscripts in the British Library, Manuscripts Collection which contain most of the letters of Horatio Nelson, Emma Hamilton, Greville Hamilton, William Hamilton, the Queen of Naples and various other key characters. These can be easily accessed by using the British Library Manuscripts Catalogue. Especially interesting are Emma's letters Add. MS 34.989 and Nelson's letters Eg MS 1614. Many of the letters have been printed in Alfred Morrison Collection, *Hamilton & Nelson Papers*, Volumes I and II, 1892, 1894 (BL shelf mark LR 4 e 1). Where available I have pointed to this printed collection of letters for easy reference in the endnotes, although I have also examined the original manuscripts where available. I have also indicated some printed editions of collection of letters for ease of use by those interested in reading more of the letters.

Manuscripts

British Library, Manuscripts Collection
- Additional (Add.) MSS
- Egerton MSS
- Spencer Papers

National Maritime Museum
- Bridport Papers
- Phillips Papers, Croker Collection
- Phillips Papers, Girdlestone Collection
- Nelson/Ward Collection

Printed Sources

Angelo, Henry, *Reminiscences of Henry Angelo* (London: 1828).

Anon, *The Letters of Lord Nelson to Lady Hamilton; with supplement of interesting letters by distinguished characters* (Thomas Lovewell & Co, London: 1814).

Anon, *Memoirs of Lady Hamilton* (Henry Colburn, London: 1815).

Anson, E and F (ed), *Mary Hamilton* (London: 1925).

Beckford, William, *Italy, Spain and Portugal* (London: 1840).

Brief Description of the cities of London & Westminster (London: 1776).

Elliot, Sir Gilbert, *Life and Letters of First Earl of Minto* (London: 1874).

Fielding, John, *An Account of the origin and effects of a Police . . . To which is added A PLAN for preserving those deserted Girls in this Town, who become prostitutes from Necessity* (London: 1758).

Foster, Vere (ed), *The Two Duchesses. Family correspondence relating to Georgiana Duchess of Devonshire, Elizabeth Duchess of Devonshire, Earl of Bristol, etc* (Blackies: London: 1898).

Goethe, Johann Wolfgang von, *Italian Journey 1786-1788,* tr W H Auden and Elizabeth Mayer (Collins, London: 1962).

Gordon, Pryse Lockhart, *Personal Memoirs* (London: 1830).

Grant, N H, *The Letters of Mary Nisbet of Dirleton, Countess of Elgin* (London: 1926).

Hanway, J, *The Defects of Police in the Cause of Immorality, and the Continual Robberies Committed, Particularly in and about the Metropolis* (London: 1775).

Harrison, James, *The Life of Lord Viscount Nelson* (London: 1806).

Hayley, William, *The Life of George Romney* (T Payne, London: 1809).

Knight, Cornelia, *Autobiography* (W H Allen, London: 1861).

Illchester, Earl of (ed), *Journal of Elizabeth, Lady Holland* (London: 1908).

Le Brun, Madame, *Memoirs of Madame Vigeé Lebrun* (Grant Richards, London: 1904).

Naish, George P B, *Nelson's Letters to his Wife and Other Documents 1785–1831* (Routledge & Kegan Paul, London: 1958).

Piozzi, Mrs Hester Lynch, *Observations and Reflections Made in the Journey through France, Italy and Germany* (London: 1789).

Pettigrew, Thomas, *Memoirs of the Life of Vice-Admiral Lord Viscount Nelson* (T & W Boone, London: 1849).

Rose, George, *Diaries and Correspondence of the Right Honourable George Rose* (Bentley, London: 1860).

Russell, Lord John (ed), *Memorials and Correspondence of Charles James Fox* (London: 1853).

Swinburne, Henry, *The Court of Europe at the Close of the Last Century* (London: 1895).

Wraxhall, Sir Nathaniel, *Historical and Personal Memoirs,* Vol I (London: 1884).

Secondary Sources
NB The best biography is by Walter Sichel.

On Emma

Bishop, Edward, *Emma Lady Hamilton* (Heron Books, 1969).

Bailey, J T, *Life of Emma Hamilton* (London: 1905).

D'Auvergne, Edmund B, *The Dear Emma* (George Harrap & Co, London: 1936).

Frankau, Julia ['Frank Danby'], *Nelson's Legacy. Lady Hamilton. Her story & Tragedy* (Cassell, London: 1915).

Frazer, Flora, *Beloved Emma* (Weidenfeld and Nicolson, London: 1986).

Hamilton, Gerald and Stewart, Desmond, *Emma In Blue* (Allan Wingate, London: 1957).

Hardwick, Mollie, *Emma, Lady Hamilton: a study* (Holt, Rinehart and Winston, New York: 1969).

Hudson, Roger (ed), *Nelson and Emma* (The Folio Society, London: 1994).

Jaffé, Patricia, *Lady Hamilton in Relation to the Art of her Time* (Arts Council, London: 1972).

Jeaffreson, John Cordy, *Beaux and Belles of England: Lady Hamilton and Lord Nelson*, Vols I and II (Athenaeum Press, London: 1897).

Lofts, Nora, *Emma Hamilton* (Book Club Associates, London: 1978).

Long, W H, *Memoirs of Emma, Lady Hamilton* (Gibbings & Co, London: 1899): a reprint of 1815 edition.

Moorhouse, E Hallam, *Nelson's Lady Hamilton* (Methuen, London: 1908).

Pocock, Tom, *Nelson's Women* (André Deutsch, London: 1999).

Russell, Jack, *Nelson and the Hamiltons* (Penguin, Harmonsworth: 1969).

Sherrard, O A, *A Life of Emma Hamilton* (Sidgewick & Jackson, London: 1927).

Sichel, Walter, *Emma Lady Hamilton* (Archibald Constable, London: 1905).

Simpson, Colin, *Emma: The Life of Lady Hamilton* (The Bodley Head, London: 1983).

Tours, Hugh, *The Life and Letters of Emma Hamilton* (V Gollancz, London: 1963).

Warner, Oliver, *Emma Hamilton and Sir William*, (Chatto & Windus, London: 1960).

On Others

Anson, E and F (eds), *Mary Hamilton* (John Murray, London: 1925).

Goethe, Johann Wolfgang (trans. W H Auden and Elizabeth Mayer), *Italian Journey 1786–1788* (Collins, London: 1962).

Coleman, Terry, *Nelson. The Man and the Legend* (Bloomsbury, London: 2001).

Connell, Brian, *Portrait of a Whig Peer* (Methuen and Co, London: 1910).

Dane, Clement (ed), *The Nelson Touch. An Anthology of Lord Nelson's Letters* (William Heinmann, London: 1942).

Fothergill, Brian, *Sir William Hamilton: Envoy Extraordinary* (Faber and Faber, London: 1969).

Gérin, Winifred, *Horatia Nelson* (Oxford University Press, Oxford & New York: 1970).

Hibbert, Christopher, *Nelson. A Personal History* (Viking, London: 1994).

Jenkins, Ian and Sloan, Kim, *Vases and Volcanoes. Sir William Hamilton and his Collection* (British Museum Press, London: 1996).

Lawrence, A W, *The Travel Letters of Lady Mary Wortley Montagu* (Jonathan Cape, London: 1930).

Meade-Fetherstonhaugh, Margaret and Warner, Oliver, *Uppark and Its People* (The National Trust, London: 1995).

Oman, Carola, *Nelson* (The Reprint Society, London: 1947).

Poole, Keith B, *The Two Beaus* (EP Publishing, Wakefield: 1976).

Rawston, Geoffrey (ed), *Nelson's Letters* (J M Dent, London: 1960).

Scholes, Percy A (ed), Charles Burney, *Musical Tours in Italy* (London: 1959).

Vincent, Edgar, *Nelson: Love & Fame* (Yale University Press, London & New Haven: 2003).

Warner, Oliver, *Nelson* (Weidenfeld and Nicolson, London: 1975).

General

Black, Jeremy, *An Illustrated History of Eighteenth-Century Britain, 1688–1793* (Manchester University Press, London: 1996).

George, Dorothy, *London Life in the Eighteenth Century* (1925, reprinted Penguin, London: 1965).

Jones, Vivien (ed), *Women in the Eighteenth Century. Constructions of Femininity* (Routledge: London, 1990).

Peakman, Julie, *Mighty Lewd Books. The Development of Pornography in Eighteenth Century England* (Palgrave, London: 2003).

_____, *Lascivious Bodies. A Sexual History of the Eighteenth century* (Atlantic, London: 2004).

Picard, Liza, *Dr Johnson's London* (Weidenfeld & Nicolson, London: 2000).

Porter, Roy, *London: A Social History* (Penguin, London: 1994).

Watson, Steven, *The Reign of George III 1760–1815* (Clarendon, Oxford: 1960).

Articles

Barbour, Judith, 'Garrick's Versions: the production of "Perdita"', *Women's Writing,* Vol 9, No 1 (2002), pp 125–38.

Gruffyd, Eirlys, 'Lord Nelson's Emma', *Buckley: The Magazine of the Buckley Society*, No 19 (Spring 1995).

Hawkes, G I, 'Emma, Lady Hamilton. Her Family and Friends on Deeside', *Buckley: The Magazine of the Buckley Society* No 21 (Spring 1997).

Wilson, Adrian, 'The Perils of Early Modern Childbirth', *British Journal for Eighteenth-Century Studies*, Vol 16, No 1 (1993).

Novels

Field, Bradda, *Bride of Glory* (Greystone Press, New York: 1942).

Kenyon, F W, *Emma* (Arrow, London: 1958).

Sontag, Susan, *The Volcano Lover* (Jonathan Cape, London: 1992).

Films

The Divine Lady (US 1929, Corrine Griffith, Victor Varconi).

Lady Hamilton (US 1941, Vivien Leigh, Laurence Olivier).

Bequest to the Nation (GB 1973, Glenda Jackson, Peter Finch).

Acknowledgements

British Library
National Maritime Museum Library
Norfolk Nelson Museum
Victory Museum, Portsmouth
Portsmouth Naval Archives & Museum
Uppark
Monmouth Museum and Archives

Picture Sources

The author and publishers wish to express their thanks to the following sources of illustrative material and/or permission to reproduce it. They will make the proper acknowledgements in future editions in the event that any omissions have occurred.

akg-Images: pp. 33, 43, 157; Clwyd Record Office: p. 5; Getty Images: pp. 26, 37, 112; Lady Lever Art Gallery: p. 121; Royal Naval Museum, Portsmouth: p. 6: Topham Picturepoint: pp. 11, 13, 16, 19, 21, 22, 45, 48, 50, 60, 61, 62, 68, 74, 78, 88, 94, 100, 102, 109, 113, 119, 125, 126, 134, 137, 140, 142, 143, 144, 161.

Index

Hamburg, 107

Hamilton, Emma: born Amy Lyon, 1, 4; appearance, 7, 39, 109–10; early employment, 7–9; first visit to London, 7–8; changes name to Emma Hart, 8; first sexual liaison, 9–10; liaison with Featherstonhaugh, 10–13; sexuality, 10, 45, 71, 161; learns to ride, 11; becomes pregnant, 12, 15; relationship with Greville, 13–20, 160; temper, 16, 19, 24, 45, 154, 160; daughter's paternity, 17–18, 24, 81, 118, 147; education and accomplishments, 19, 25, 35, 53; kindness and generosity, 19, 55, 145, 147, 151; singing, 20, 35, 49, 53, 54, 57, 61, 105, 117; sits for Romney, 20–1, 23, 60, 62; suffers urticaria, 23, 135; passed over to Hamilton, 28–30, 33–5, 38–41; sexual health, 29; passion for admiration, 30; arrives in Naples, 30–1; pragmatic character, 35; resentment towards Greville, 38; relationship with Hamilton, 44–6, 56, 71, 90, 98, 160; Attitudes, 47–9, 51, 57, 60–2, 107, 112, 161; accent, 49–50; admired in Naples, 52, 55–6; climbs Vesuvius, 54; seeks marriage, 56–8; reception in England, 59–62; marriage, 62, 149; returns to Naples, 63; received by Queen, 63–6; need for respectability, 64, 105; lack of pretensions, 66; nurses Hamilton, 67; relationship with Maria Carolina, 68, 77–81, 85, 102, 107, 141; vulgarity, 69–70, 103, 107, 149; takes up botany, 70; meets Nelson, 75–6; puts on weight, 78, 103, 107, 109–10, 149; political activities, 79–80, 84–5, 101, 161; sense of drama, 79, 83, 82, 161; praises Nelson, 86–7; effect on Nelson, 88–90, 96–7; nurses Nelson, 89; *ménage à trois* established, 90, 98, 104, 108–11; escape from Naples, 91–3, 95–6, 161; gambling, 96–7, 137; drinking, 96, 113, 149–50, 154, 158; returns to Naples, 99–101; receives gifts from Maria Carolina, 102, 107; sexual relationship with Nelson, 103–4, 117–18, 137, 160; return to England, 105–7; pregnant by Nelson, 105, 110; subject of critical attacks, 107; visits Fonthill, 111–12; Nelson's daughter born, 113–15; letters destroyed, 115; evades Prince of Wales, 116–17; poem for Nelson, 122–3; nurses Edward Parker, 123; establishes household in Merton, 124–5, 127–8; extravagance, 125, 129, 134, 136; and Hamilton's death, 131–2; seeks pension, 133, 149, 154; second child dies, 134–5; clashes with Horatia, 136, 154–6; and Nelson's departure, 139; inheritance and financial difficulties, 141, 145–51; last letter from Nelson, 142; and Nelson's death, 144–5; moves to Richmond, 149; last letter from Little Emma, 151–2; her will,

150, 153; in debtor's prison, 153

Nelson, Horatio: praise for Emma's
mother, 6; describes Naples, 32;
arrives in Naples, 71–2; family,
73, 75; liaisons, 75; appearance,
75, 76, 103; idealism, 75; meets
Emma and Hamilton, 75–6;
victory at Cape St Vincent, 83;
promoted Rear Admiral, 84;
victory at Nile, 85, 86–7;
ennobled, 87; Emma's effect on
him, 88, 90, 96–7; nursed by
Emma, 89; *ménage à trois*
established, 90, 98, 104, 110–11;
and evacuation of Naples, 91–3,
161; his will, 98, 115, 122, 129,
136, 141, 146; returns to Naples
and executes rebels, 99–100;
awarded Dukedom of Bronte,
102; rewarded by British
government, 102–3; sexual
relationship with Emma, 103–4,
117–18, 137, 160; recalled to
Britain, 105; child by Emma,
105, 110; subject of critical
attacks, 107; given hero's
welcome, 108; visits Fonthill,
111–12; promoted Vice Admiral,
112; delighted with daughter,
114–15, 119; jealous of Prince of
Wales, 116; relations with Fanny,
119–20; financial problems, 120;
victory at Copenhagen, 122–3;
resides at Merton, 123, 126–8;
takes seat in Lords, 126; and
father's death, 128–9; failing
health, 129, 135; recalled to
duty, 133; and death of second
child, 134–5; departure for
Trafalgar, 138–9; Battle of
Trafalgar and death, 141–3

Nelson, Maurice, 73, 127

Nelson, Sarah (née Yonge, later
Countess), 73; friendship with
Emma, 119, 123, 126, 127, 129,
135, 139; continuing relations
with Emma, 145, 147; son
dies, 148

Nelson, Suckling, 73

Nelson, William (later Earl), 73;
friendship with Emma, 123, 127,
129, 135, 139; inheritance and
subsequent treatment of Emma,
145–7, 157–8; son dies, 148

Ness, 4

Neston, 4

Netherlands, 69, 82

Nevis, 75

Newcombe, Frederick, 148

Nile, Battle of the, 85, 86–7,
89, 156

Nisbet, Josiah, 75, 76, 89–90

Norfolk, 73, 135

Norfolk, Duke of, 113

North Sea, 97

nunneries, 53

O'Kelly, Colonel, 156

Oxford, 129

Palazzo Sessa, 33, 35, 48, 55,
89, 99

Palermo, 93, 95–8, 101–5; feast of
St Rosalia celebrations, 102

Palmerston, Henry Temple, Lord,
36, 63–4, 109–10

Palmerston, Lady Mary, 63–4, 69

Paris, 31, 63, 70, 78, 88

Parker, Edward, 123

Parker, Sir Hyde, 113, 115

Alexander the Great
by Nigel Cawthorne
'moves through the career at a brisk,
dependable canter in his pocket
biography for Haus.'
BOYD TONKIN, *The Independent*
ISBN 1-904341-56-X (pb) £9.99

Armstrong
by David Bradbury
'it is a fine and well-researched
introduction'
GEORGE MELLY *Daily Mail*
ISBN 1-904341-46-2 (pb) £8.99

Bach
by Martin Geck
'The production values of the book
are exquisite.' *Guardian*
ISBN 1-904341-16-0 (pb) £8.99
ISBN 1-904341-35-7 (hb) £12.99

Beethoven
by Martin Geck
'...this little gem is a truly handy reference.' *Musical Opinion*
ISBN 1-904341-00-4 (pb) £8.99
ISBN 1-904341-03-9 (hb) £12.99

Bette Davis
by Laura Moser
'The author compellingly unearths the complex, self-destructive woman that lay beneath the steely persona of one of the best-loved actresses of all time.'
ISBN 1-904341-48-9 (pb) £9.99

Bevan
by Clare Beckett
and Francis Beckett
"Haus, the enterprising new imprint, adds another name to its list of short biographies ... a timely contribution.'
GREG NEALE, *BBC History*
ISBN 1-904341-63-2 (pb) £9.99

Brahms
by Hans A Neunzig
'These handy volumes fill a gap in the market for readable, comprehensive and attractively priced biographies admirably.'
JULIAN HAYLOCK, *Classic fm*
ISBN 1-904341-17-9 (pb) £8.99

Caravaggio
by Patrick Hunt
'a first-class, succinct but comprehensive,
introduction to the artist'
BRIAN TOVEY *The Art Newspaper*
ISBN 1-904341-73-X (pb) £9.99
ISBN 1-904341-74-8 (hb) £12.99

Roger Casement
by Angus Mitchell
'hot topic' *The Irish Times*
ISBN 1-904341-41-1 (pb) £8.99

Curie
by Sarah Dry
'... this book could hardly be bettered'
New Scientist
selected as
Outstanding Academic Title by *Choice*
ISBN 1-904341-29-2 (pb) £8.99

Dali
by Linde Salber
'a fascinating view on this flamboyant
artist, the central and most excentric figure
in Surrealism, seen through the prism
of psychological analysis'
ISBN 1-904341-75-6 (pb) £9.99

Dietrich
by Malene Sheppard Skærved
'It is probably the best book ever on Marlene.' CHRISTOPHER DOWNES
ISBN 1-904341-13-6 (pb) £8.99

Dostoevsky
by Richard Freeborn
'wonderful ... a learned guide'
JOHN CAREY *The Sunday Times*
ISBN 1-904341-27-6 (pb) £8.99

Dvořák
by Kurt Honolka
'This book seems really excellent to me.'
SIR CHARLES MACKERRAS
ISBN 1-904341-52-7 (pb) £9.99

Einstein
by Peter D Smith
'Concise, complete, well-produced and lively throughout, ... a bargain at the price.' *New Scientist*
ISBN 1-904341-14-4 (hb) £12.99
ISBN 1-904341-15-2 (pb) £8.99

Gershwin
by Ruth Leon
'Musical theatre aficionados will relish Ruth Leon's GERSHWIN, a succinct but substantial account of the great composer's life'
MICHAEL ARDITTI, *The Independent*
ISBN 1-904341-23-3 (pb) £9.99

Johnson
by Timothy Wilson Smith
'from a prize-winning author a biography of the famous and perennially fascinating figure, Samuel Johnson'
ISBN 1-904341-81-0 (pb) £9.99

Joyce
by Ian Pindar
'I enjoyed the book very much, and much approve of this skilful kind of popularisation. It reads wonderfully well.'
TERRY EAGLETON
ISBN 1-904341-58-6 (pb) £9.99

Kafka
by Klaus Wagenbach
'one of the most useful books on Kafka ever published.' New Scientist
ISBN 1-904341-01-2 (hb) £12.99
ISBN 1-904341-02-0 (pb) £8.99

Moreschi, The Last Castrato
by Nicholas Clapton
'an immaculately produced and beautifully
illustrated short volume ... Clapton
is excellent on the physical and psychological
effects of castration as experienced
by Moreschi.'
ANDREW GREEN, *Classical Music*
ISBN 1-904341-77-2 (pb) £9.99

Mosley
by Nigel Jones
'an excellent brief life of Britain's 1930s
Fascist leader ... Jones does manage to get
a more accurate view of Mosley than some
previous, weightier books.'
FRANCIS BECKETT, *Jewish Chronicle*
ISBN 1-904341-09-8 (pb) £9.99

Welles
by Ben Walters
'the book works well as an introduction
to Welles's work' *Sunday Telegraph*
ISBN 1-904341-80-2 (pb) £9.99

Wilde
by Jonathan Fryer
'Fryer has a great gift for finding the pertinent
quotation. His analysis of the relation
between the man and the dramatist is
sharp and convincing.'
Independent on Sunday
ISBN 1-904341-11-X (pb) £9.99